Duncan

Food for your thoughts.

Geoff.

Before It's Too Late

A Very Ordinary Citizen's Manifesto

Aka Geoff Feasey's Jottings

CW00840493

ISBN: 978-1-326-29591-2

The photograph on the cover is of two of the author's 'Scrapwood Sculptures'. They represent Chaos and Order and remind us that although we may have views on Life, the Universe and Almost Everything, those views should add up to a clear direction of travel for us all, leading to a sustainable world.

Photograph by Squib Photography Ltd whose expertise was much appreciated

Introduction

Why write a personal manifesto? Partly: for fun. More seriously, having occasionally been dubbed a 'dangerous pinko' by conservative naval colleagues, and now living in deep blue west Oxfordshire, I want to set out my thoughts to see whether they make sense.

Of course, it will not be a proper manifesto. It is obvious that weighty books have been devoted to most of the complex topics considered. However, all decisions on what to think, believe and do, must be reduced to a binary choice in the end: 'To be or not to be' says it all.

My views and the anecdotes chosen to illustrate points are therefore mercilessly squashed into a few paragraphs. Even so, I hope they will promote exchange of ideas, not least because I've observed that sometimes seemingly hard-core Tories - some of my best friends are Conservatives - have liberal, sometimes even egalitarian, values below the surface.

The manifesto was outlined in July 2011 with the sub-title 'Geoff's Jottings'. They have now been updated and expanded because much has changed since then, especially as the evidence for climate change suggests a need for greater awareness at the ordinary citizen's level.

Finally: in one or two cases, I may be able to add a thought, based on long experience, which is not in the text books.

Point of View

Emigration to Australia in 1979 and life there had a profound effect on my thinking. After I returned to and settled 'permanently' in England in 2002, I looked, and still look, at the UK through Australian eyes with much that that implies. And my look at the evidence of life around the world and my reading have led me to some fundament conclusions.

My family were not churchgoers and I learned little about religion during childhood but joining the navy broadened my horizons. I met many good, kindly, religious people and admiration for them led me to join their ranks. I began to study theology and was even encouraged to consider whether I had a 'calling' to the Methodist ministry. However, study and books such as 'Honest to God' soon separated the goodness of individuals from the theology and power structures of various denominations. And the evidence suggested that if there is an omnipresent, omniscient and omnipotent god, he or she is certainly not just the loving God of 'All Things Bright and Beautiful' but also, for some ineffable reason, the vicious creator of 'All Things Vile and Venomous'. So now I am an atheist, a 'six' on the Dawkins scale. Nevertheless, I cherish goodness and try to tolerate the faith of others, unless of course they want to kill me because I am not of their flock!

The Fundamentals of Life

Regardless of what individuals believe, the historical and contemporary evidence is overwhelming: most communities, be they primitive or sophisticated, wish to have a system of faith in something beyond this life usually something supernatural. Nevertheless, I believe that whether we like it or not, we are simply animal creatures, fortunate to be living on a planet which happens to be in a 'Goldilocks Zone', not too hot, not too cold, just right for life as we know it to develop, but vulnerable to exploitation. We are not here because some supernatural being placed us in charge for ever and ever amen.

In the absence of divine guidance, we must get to grips with the realities of our world. Why are we here? Answer: stop looking for an answer. We just *are* here and should be thankful for that. Thankful too that provided we take care of it, our world can be quite a good place in which to live. And, most importantly, even though some mammals have bigger brains than ours, we have the best developed brains of all the animals on earth. So although our genes impose a fundamental duty on us to secure the future of our species, all sorts of options on how to live are open to us.

One of the most important decisions we must make, individually and collectively, is where to place ourselves on the spectrum from selfish, devil take the hindmost, survival of the fittest, to idealistic, sharing, caring altruism for the common good. Competition or cooperation? Hopefully we can find some practical options!

The next major fundamental that we must not forget is that the planet's resources are finite. There are plenty of areas in the world where we can observe animal populations expanding in the good times until along comes a drought, earthquake or other natural event. Then the food runs out and unless there is human intervention herds and flocks die of starvation until the balance between population and food supply is restored – until next time! Our highly developed, mainly urban, societies should not forget the basics of the bush.

Finally, one of the most significant driving forces of our animal natures is *power*. From the male dominating weaker mates in the jungle and the symbiosis of Church and Nobility dominating the peasantry, sometimes symbolised by the cosy proximity of castles and churches along the Danube and Rhine, to the ruthless determination of some present day businesses to dominate their market at all costs, power is sought and valued. We would be wise to restrain the grab for it.

Fundamentals beget Problems

I have never liked the trendy "There are no problems, only opportunities". Identifying the problems affecting people's lives is a good starting point for politicians and managers. International problems are different in kind so it's convenient to list them separately even though they affect the solutions to our homespun problems.

The international ones include: climate change; increasing population; resource depletion; affluent wellbeing, sometimes obscenely affluent, in the developed world; hunger; poverty and deprivation elsewhere; oppression by tyrants; traditional enmities; the threat of terrorism, religious fanaticism and, omnipresent, human nature.

At home in Britain, it would be easy to produce an endless list, depending on what is regarded as a problem. For instance, should the volatility of Stock Exchange share prices and their vulnerability to computerised manipulation be regarded as a problem, or just a fact of modern life? Best, I think, just to highlight the most basic problems affecting or threatening to affect many people, leaving others to be considered later.

So, regardless of the nature, importance and urgency of each: an increasing population which is increasingly obese and increasingly aged; an appalling shortage of affordable housing; shortage of jobs; the increasing gulf between rich and poor; historic tensions between labour and management; residual 'class' differences which hinder social mobility; an unhelpful culture of confrontation in parliament, the courts and industry; the defensive secrecy of some public service officials; and an ill maintained infrastructure inadequate for the needs of a mixed population of indigenous and immigrant ethnic groups that have not merged into a comfortable, multicultural society. Plenty to go on with!

Now, about the UK. Where to start?

My first impressions on return to the UK in 2002 were – leaving aside the appalling state of the roads and pavements - of a country awash with money: or at least credit. The 'haves' taking two or three holidays a year with some 'short breaks' in between, often to overseas destinations; many of the 'have-nots' sharing similar expectations even though they didn't have the means to fulfil their desires; shopping as the favourite hobby of many young women, and increasingly, young men; these and other indications showed it was definitely not the Britain I left in 1979.

Next impression: this new world is encouraging many people to work harder to earn more money to spend going places, buying things and generally consuming. This makes companies rich but gives many families a thoroughly bad work/life balance which many complain about but too often seem to be unable to resist. By comparison, I think it's still true to say that most Aussies know why they should work hard: it's so they can have plenty of shrimps on the barbie at the weekend.

And after the first impressions? Not necessarily a 'broken country' as Prime Minister David Cameron suggested, in many ways not even a backward country, but certainly a backward-looking country clinging to the last vestiges of greatness, apparently forgetting that the Great in Great Britain referred to the union, not to the UK's power in the world, great though that was in the 19th and early 20th centuries.

The evidence for this backward-looking? A simple example of clinging to the past is the failure to complete metrication. Even though it is over forty years since it became government policy to introduce the SI system of units, and the metrication manuals landed on my desk, the UK still lives in a mishmash of Imperial and metric. And NASA's space programme experience showed how risky that can be. There are many other examples. In 2004 the government invited people to suggest money saving changes they might implement. It was easy to respond: my submission proposed completing metrication and twelve other measures. Only one has been implemented.

Observation of government action and inaction has been backed by the responses to conversations and the straw polls I've conducted, and the frequently predictable, inarticulate responses of the citizens-in-the-street to radio and television interviewers' questions on life, the universe or anything – not to mention some of the wilder comments on the social media. They often indicate a wilful resistance to change, even a longing to rewind the calendar a few decades.

Why is anyone thinking like that? Perhaps the root cause is that although primary education became available for all with the passing of the Education Act of 1870, too many people have still not been given, partially for religious and partly for social class reasons, an understanding of the basic nature of our life on earth: probabilistic and animal, but nevertheless potentially very enjoyable. Many people today, especially older ones, are therefore unable to understand and cope with the ups and the many downs of life in Britain today. All too often we hear, "I'm too old for all that", an expression rarely heard in Australia.

The people of Britain exhibit behaviour not seen in earlier decades. Examples are the adulation of football players and so-called celebrities; the wild mood swings when national teams win a medal or two, or lose; the hysterical acclamations of television studio and theatre audiences; the self indulgent excesses at the death of Diana.

These behavioural trends co-exist with widespread disregard for the laws intended to ensure civilised living in town and country. And although many people tell me that life is far too hectic these days, few show any inclination to do much to decrease the tempo. They are too busy trying to live up to their materialistic expectations at a time of record national and personal debt and a widening gulf between have-lots and have-littles.

Is the state of the nation really so bad? Is the glass half full or half empty? Engineers are trained to deal with problems so we tend to concentrate on what is wrong, taking for granted all the things that are OK. Yes, Britain has tremendous talent – and I don't mean for singing pop songs - but so much is wrong.

Some examples. Failure to use the North Sea oil tax revenues to update the nation's infrastructure: did the nation enjoy a spending spree instead? Short-sightedly electing to encourage service industries instead of supporting manufacturing; a wrong decision of recent years which is now being adjusted. Failure to persuade workers that if we didn't introduce modern manufacturing methods to build ships, planes and cars the world would leave us behind. Even in areas where we still excel, our companies are often under foreign ownership and leadership, with all the vulnerability that that entails. And we have failed to develop a technologically-savvy civil service capable of introducing government IT systems as efficient as those of our best supermarkets.

More recently: government policies, insufficiently challenged by media or public, involve contradictions such as 'decisions should be made locally' but 'there must not be a post-code lottery'. Every day seems to reveal new evidence. As I write this there is the silliness of continuing to pay the salary of a Member of Parliament while he is serving a jail sentence for fraud: a small example but a telling one.

How unpleasant can life in UK become? Much worse, as indicated by the riots, fires and looting of recent years, the malicious use of social media, the political and social impacts of immigration, the ever widening rich/poor gap, and external influences and threats. There is cause for serious concern almost every day. As I write today it is the tax evasion/avoidance activities of HSBC: who knows what rebellious thoughts that demonstration of the power of wealth might trigger in someone's mind? It does not much matter whether academics, analysts or journalists correctly describe the detailed causes: in a well organised community. there simply should not be any reason for such responses whether to national or overseas influences.

There are also longer term factors of which I only became aware after I returned to the UK and started reading more about the Thatcher/Blair years. For instance, although the sale of council houses was reported by the Australian media, I hadn't seen any reference to the prohibition preventing councils from recycling funds and building replacements, which paved the way for the abysmal lack of affordable housing today. Reading of the politics, economics and social history of recent times confirmed my belief that whether broken, or just damaged, Britain needs a wake-up call.

It's time to sort ourselves out. A shock treatment might be a suitable symbolic act with which to start.

The Shock Treatment.

First, establish a more equal society. Taxation to redistribute wealth? No, something much more fundamental to reawaken the British people. Abolish the monarchy, the aristocracy and the orders of knighthood. Create a society in which everyone except convicted felons can say, like Bluntschli in George Bernard Shaw's 'Arms and the Man', that they belong to the highest stratum of their country: Free Citizen. That would provide a vastly more encouraging basis for the future than the remnants of a feudal system.

The abolition of the monarchy would send a powerful message: Brits are not subjects! Our passports no longer refer to all of us as subjects (though some people are still subjects – see note 2 of your passport). Most of us have been promoted to citizens so why retain the Monarchy with all the undemocratic bowing and scraping? Two main reasons of course.

First, most thinking people recognise the value of the reserve powers of the Monarch as Head of State: no quick bit of legislation and a "Prime Minister for Life" in Britain thank you very much. However, reserve powers could be conferred equally effectively on a non-executive President. Better, some Australians would argue. When Queen Elizabeth was asked in 1975 to use her powers to dismiss the elected Prime Minister of Australia, she declined to act and left it to her representative, the Governor General. There's passing the buck!

Second, the ceremonial surrounding the monarchy has become the (arguably very expensive) anchor of our tourist business. True but unwise. Tourism, like many service industries, is easily abandoned when political or natural instability frightens people or when resource shortages send prices soaring. Furthermore, there is evidence that tourism fares equally well in republics: the queues at Versailles are often quoted as an example.

Without the Monarchy there would be no basis for an aristocracy in which a few enjoy privileges earned by their forebears, sometimes centuries earlier, but for which there is no longer any rational justification. Unearned privilege occurs at various levels of British life: even a simple thing like commissioned officer status in the armed services was a fairly widespread example until recently, and it is still encountered occasionally.

Then there are the Dukedoms with their Blenheims and Chatswoods, and all the rest! Eliminating their titles and those of the orders of knighthood would send a very strong signal that henceforth privilege must be earned, and when earned, should be borne modestly. Services to the nation can always, and should always, be recognised, but without conferring fancy titles. What will happen to their palaces, estates and vast landholdings? Read on, that comes later.

By this stage some readers may be thinking, 'The wretched fellow's a communist and we all know how badly communism failed'. No, I'm just a 'little-s socialist', and I'll mention later what I mean by that. However, I do believe western nations succumbed too wholeheartedly to hubris when the USSR collapsed. There was little of Churchill's 'In victory, magnanimity', too much 'We kicked ass. We won'.

It had certainly been demonstrated that it is impossible to impose the ethos of a commune on a transcontinental empire of hundreds of millions of people, especially when opposed by the immense wealth and industrial power of the western nations.

However, when the USSR collapsed, those western nations gave little publicity to any regrets like those of some Hungarian teachers, recorded by A P Riemer in

'The Habsburg Café'. Although the teachers may have detested Soviet domination, they recognised that although they had little wealth under that system, life was actually better then than after capitalism suddenly exploded into gross inequalities. Because it was fair!

"Equal misery for all" may not be an elegant zeitgeist but many people find it satisfying if everyone shares good times and bad In the bad they may call it 'The Dunkirk Spirit' and conveniently, sentimentally, forget that during World War 2 there were many inequalities of attitude, opportunity and suffering.

If not a commie, a revolutionary perhaps? No, I'll drink the Loyal Toast with a clear conscience partly because I wish our dutiful Queen what I would wish anyone, good health and happiness during the remaining years of her life, but also because a longer version of the toast is 'The Queen and Her Heirs and Successors at Law'. An orderly legislative progress from Monarchy to Republic would be fine.

Charlie Windsor-Wales will then be free to express himself in whatever way he wishes. William and Kate Windsor-Wales will be free to really earn their living as they seem well capable of doing. And we shall all find that, as most Australians are already aware from their experience of excellent Governors General, a President could be a far better leader for the nation: and much cheaper!

Becoming a republic.

A written constitution?   These are rarely perfect, especially when lawyers get to work. A classic example is Section 92 the Australian Constitution entitled 'Trade within the Commonwealth to be free'. After some interim arrangements there are only 28 more words and their intention seems to be clear: no customs posts at state borders. Simple? We might think so but I'm told books have been written on the meaning of those few words.

Flaws in written constitutions can have serious consequences. I lived in Malta when Prime Minister Mintoff wanted to turn the country into a republic. The Constitution was scanned.   It had entrenched clauses which could be changed only by a two thirds majority in Parliament – an unlikely happening in strongly partisan Malta – and clauses for which a simple majority in Parliament would suffice. Surprise: the simple clause which made the Constitution superior to Parliament was not entrenched. Quick vote in Parliament, all legal, job done. Moral: always be very, very careful with the drafting!

It's hard to imagine a republic without a written Constitution. It makes so much more sense to contain any wayward party politicians by having one: interpreted by a small court of trusted judges in whom the public have confidence; and only to be amended by referenda. I'm confident the Australians, Canadians and Americans would be pleased to help. If backward looking traditionalists try to persuade Britain to continue without one, suspect that they may be trying to preserve the privileges of The Establishment: unless they can produce an unassailable case they should be ignored.

Since writing that I have become aware of, and in a small way participated in, the invitation from the LSE's Institute of Public Affairs to the public to participate in, advise on, and eventually contribute to a draft written Constitution for the UK. How's that for a step towards real democracy?

After abolishing the monarchy, how do we select our President? The referendum on whether Australia should become a republic made people aware of some relevant issues. An executive President like the US or a non-executive with reserve powers limited by the Constitution? A President elected by popular vote of all the people? Or by a two thirds majority in both Houses of Parliament after nomination by the Prime Minister of the day? Or some similar formula?

There seems little doubt that countries accustomed to a Westminster-style government would find an executive President unacceptable: the thought of a system which might produce a George W Bush clone should be enough to dispose of that option.

The remaining election questions are easily settled by asking 'Who would want to stand for election as President by popular vote?' Almost certainly, only politicians, whereas the parliamentary alternative could draw upon many fine business leaders, academics, judges, retired officers of the armed services and others, like those who have served Australia so well as Governors General. There are many variations on election procedures but the principle is clear: choose a scheme which offers the prospect of finding good men and women who are above party politics – they do exist!

Reform titles and honours. Follow the abolition of royal and aristocratic titles by ceasing to confer medieval knighthoods on those who have served their country well: let their honour be recognised by a discrete buttonhole badge, brooch or something similar. Restrict titles to the practical ones: Professor, Admiral, Doctor, etc. And I might mischievously suggest sneaking in one new one: 'Engineer'. Or would that be a step too far for a country which finds it hard to differentiate between professional engineers, technicians and mechanics?

What about Parliament? Experience suggests there is little value (though perhaps some entertainment at Prime Minister's Question Time) in some aspects of present practice. The House of Commons is an unwieldy vehicle for debating bills; most of the useful debate therefore occurs in committee. The first-past-the-post system of voting promotes a two party adversarial system and the structure of the chamber is designed to reflect this. And the archaic system of voting lobbies wastes a lot of valuable time.

It is a pity that the recent Conservative/Liberal Democrat coalition's referendum failed to favour a system which more proportionately reflects the preferences of the electorate. However reform of voting for MPs would probably have not done much good without radical reform of our antiquated, adversarial parliamentary system and associated voting practice. Instant electronic voting is the most obvious example of a need which could be satisfied easily and relatively cheaply. Less easy would be a reduction in the number of MPs with the intention of fostering less adversarial, more rational, debate. To put it more generally, in future the parliament should neither be bogged down by tradition nor treated as a club by any of its members.

An 'Upper' House? No, not 'upper' but yes, certainly, provided it is an effective 'house of review', a 'second opinion', not a haven for superannuated party politicians from the Commons. To be as effective as possible it should combine the talents of elected representatives and appointees who bring their specialist knowledge and experience to the debates.

Why should we vote for two kinds of representative? Simply because experience elsewhere proves the worth of elected representatives who bring a different, broader attitude to public affairs than those who stand as constituency members, most of whom, nowadays, have entered party politics fresh from university. That experience also shows that good people, who wouldn't dream of joining the bear pit of the Commons, will stand for election and bring their experience to bear on legislation as, and there probably isn't a better title, Senators. Experts assure us that there are plenty of voting systems which would help differentiate between voting for MPs and for Senators.

Friends have reminded me that Australian experience tells us that the Senate system can be misused. A particular State may be favoured to get legislation passed: but any system can be abused. We only have to study the behaviour of the House of Lords before reform to see that.

What about the Bishops? There is no justification whatever for a privileged position for an established Church of England in twenty-first century British life. It follows that if there is to be any representation of religions in parliament it should at the most be proportionately similar to that of professions and other specialist groups in the house of review. More on religion later.

What else? We should certainly get rid of the 'Upper', 'Lower' and 'Commons' titles! And with an improved electoral system we might think of getting rid of the adversarial layout of the houses. The Scots have shown us the way. And I must now add that it has recently been stated that vastly expensive repairs needed by the Houses of Parliament might make it more sensible to knock them down and build anew.

Reforming 'The Establishment'. Accompanying the far reaching constitutional changes there would be myriad matters requiring attention, from the abolition of any kind of Privy Council to the (very unlikely) need for a Governor General's Warrant on a jar of jam. An impossible task? I suggest not.

Some voices are likely to suggest that it's bound to be impossible! They would most likely be the voice of 'The Establishment', seeking, as has happened so often in the past, to delay change and preserve unwarranted privilege or power. If we regard it as a great opportunity to get rid of the accumulated dross of ages it could be the beginning of a new era of soundly based national pride. The primary requirement to make it happen? Resolute leadership which brooks no half measures or backward glances.

When the Shock Treatment is completed and Britain begins to look ahead. What next? It might be convenient to think about the way ahead under three headings: The Planet; Our Place in the World; and Organising our Country. Inevitably, they are all interconnected. That's life!

The Planet

Years ago when I began to learn about climate change, the situation could be summed up, crudely compressed, as follows. Scientific evidence suggested that there is a threat to our future on this planet. The scientists, not surprisingly, could not be precise about severity or timescale. Prudence should have convinced nations and their populations to take out insurance by 'Thinking globally. Acting locally'. Some of us began to do so. The governments of the world were far less prudent.

The scientific evidence is becoming ever more robust. However, the pace of international action has been severely limited by several factors: entrenched scepticism, the difficulties of adapting the Western capitalist system to abnormal circumstances; the interactions between the rich nations that contributed most to the threat and the aspirations of poor nations seeking to raise the living standards of their people.

Some years have passed since 2015 was identified as the earliest 'tipping point' at which a rise of 2 degrees in the average temperature might signal an irreversible change in the climate of our world. 2015 is now here – I'm pleased I have survived to see it – and although there is plenty of evidence of global warming, there is no indication of immediate doom.

Instead the situation appears to be that the best estimate of earth's limit for coping with carbon dioxide in the atmosphere without increasing global warming more than 2 degrees is one trillion tonnes. Of that vast amount a half is reported to have already entered the atmosphere, and at the present rate of increase the limit is forecast to be reached in less than 40 years. A convincing case I would have thought, for accelerated international action but there is little evidence of a will to grasp the problem.

Nevertheless, it is possible to choose, as individuals and as individual nations, prudent lifestyles which allow adjustments promoting people's wellbeing, happiness, call it what you will, and yet safeguard the future against the threats of resource depletion and catastrophic, unstoppable, global warming. Nationally and internationally, we must try to find a new and happier balance of life, work and ecological footprint.

Britain's Place in the World

There's no doubt that Britain was once great. Nor doubt that greatness diminished from the beginning of the twentieth century, reaching the low level of international influence which depressed Churchill at the time of the Yalta Summit. Greatness has gone.

The trouble is that no one seems to have told the British people to forget yearnings for past glories – if that's what they were - and to settle down and rejoice that Britain still has so many assets that it could be very happy in the role of a medium size, well organised country.

One example of the pointlessness of exaggerated ambition was the assumption in the nineteen fifties that Britain should have its own, comprehensive, space programme, an ambition soon shown to be unrealistic. So we became part of the European Space Programme which enabled us to share influence beyond the means of any single European country and to use Britain's ample brains to contribute experiments and equipment for national and international projects.   A reminder that we should have more modest ambitions?

More recently voices, sometimes strident, have been raised recently to protest against possible cuts to the World Service of the BBC: 'The world relies on us for the truth'. Whether that is true or false is not the question. It is 'when will the British taxpayer realise that it is no longer Britain's responsibility to broadcast truth to the world?'   We can choose whether we wish to do so.

And when our British government proposes projects such as the London to Birmingham TGV, known to us as HS2, we should think hard about them. Is it really worth the financial and social costs?   Or is it just a wish to keep up with the French and other Europeans? Do we feel we would lose face because we live in a crowded little island and cannot easily accommodate the gentle curves required by super-fast trains?

Recent history, especially of the Iraq war, points to the wisdom of defining a more modest role for Britain in relation to the rest of the world, one without illusions of greatness. In doing so we should resist the temptation to apply double standards: one for people we like and another for the rest. We should avoid opportunism: challenging brutal dictatorships after tolerating them for decades because for instance, we had a commercial interest at stake.

However, it's not easy for a country to give up illusions of power and influence. Australia went 'All the way with LBJ' to Vietnam and regretted it. The words 'never again' were often voiced; but apparently not heard because Australia again succumbed to the call of the US to join later Gulf wars.

There's no doubt that Britain too was under considerable pressure from the US to join the Vietnam War but showed strength by refusing to join it. It can be done. It should be done unless there is an overwhelming UN case for intervention in another nation' affairs to which all possible countries contribute their share.

Is the Special Relationship with the USA one of those illusions of influence? A cold hard look at the evidence suggests, not surprisingly, that the USA only operates in its own best, world wide interests. They can behave harshly towards any nation that dares offend them: ask how the US responded when the Kiwis wanted assurances about nuclear weapons in US warships visiting NZ ports. The Australian sheep industry was invited to advise their US counterpart in expanding their business, not so easy in what has long been a 'cattle country'. I've been told they were rewarded by in import surcharge on Australian sheep meat. It's best not expect much from the Special Relationship.

An Economist leader of 1981 suggested (perhaps quoting Bagehot?) that 'Government should begin with a symbol and move on to action'. That sounded like a good idea. For example, Britain could seek an agreement with Argentina to share sovereignty of the Falklands Islands. If achieved, that really would show a bit of world leadership: how to solve, peacefully, a centuries old dispute, while at the same time symbolising a new British world view in which we have no illusions but stand up for ourselves as a self confident, modest nation

But why should we share Falklands sovereignty? That question will certainly be asked, especially by those who gallantly defended it. We are told the islanders wish to remain British, tourism is being promoted, exploration for oil is licensed in the area.

The thinking behind my answer is explored later under the heading of Principle and Pragmatism. As a matter of principle we should respect the wishes of the islanders. But what if disease wipes out all but a dozen of them? Should the British taxpayer still pay for a garrison of 1,200 (soon to be increased I hear) to defend the islands? Do Argentina's taxpayers wish to contribute to possible future military adventures by their government? Could we not jointly define suitable terms for operations by the oil industry? Would it really make much difference to their operations? Do they really care, provided the work for which they are licensed can be done without hindrance? It could be a win-win for both countries and the savings could fund generous compensation for any islanders who wish to leave.

Our armed services might complain that they would lose valuable training areas. But training for what? Defence, another factor in determining Britain's place in the world will be considered later. Before that we'd better think about our economy which greatly affects our options for finding our position in the world.

The Economy: Capitalism and Markets

Why consider economics with particular reference to capitalism and the markets? Simply because we do not have a blank sheet of paper on which to draw up a new system. We must start with the existing, so called, democratic capitalist system and with our need to find solutions for our problems with homes, jobs, welfare, pensions etc.

I've always been grateful to the Institution of Mechanical Engineers for insisting that the Admiralty include Economics of Engineering in the education of engineer officers. Microeconomics stimulated an interest in the complex world of macroeconomics, capitalism and the markets, even though that world has to be reduced to some simple ideas to make much sense to me. That's because it seems to me that in Western nations two systems are operating all the time.

Of two fundamentals I'm certain. First, in a capitalist system, in the absence of regulation of one kind or another, wealth converges. At the individual level this is because, contrary to the generalisation in the Declaration of Independence of the United States, men are not created equal. The Founding Fathers should have taken more notice of the parable of the talents in Matthew's and Luke's Gospels which told of widely different responses to investment. That range of responses, accompanied in some cases by the human propensity for greed, soon allows certain individuals to collar more than an average share of the loot. Then, after their survival-needs have been met, they are free to spend, save, invest, gamble or even to become respected philanthropists.

And second, in any production system there is an inevitable gap: between seed-time and harvest, between tooling-up for production and sales, between trading across the world and pocketing the proceeds in the home port. Time lags such as these, combined with the variability of nature and other factors, cause producers to need credit. Those clever with money supply it. And capitalism is born.

Is that bad? No, not inherently. Antonio didn't whinge when his enterprises failed and Shylock sought his pound of flesh. To bear unexpected failure with fortitude and success with equanimity is reasonable. But troubles creep in when, in the absence of adequate regulation, gambling replaces investment. The haves might argue, 'I have the means, why should I not gamble?' No reason at all provided they do so with their own money. But every reason why - bankers in particular - shouldn't be allowed to gamble with anyone else's, especially if they are entrusted with the pension savings of those who have only a slender margin of income above their survival-level needs.

Is money the only factor? In their book 'The Lessons of History' Will and Ariel Durrant described war as 'a constant of history'. Others might have written about another constant: greed. Greed manifests itself in all sorts of ways but a common factor is that it allows humans to disregard concern for others. To complicate matters further, some learned economists from Keynes to Akerlof and Shiller accept that classical economic theory cannot cope with 'animal spirits', (otherwise known as human nature?), which make humans prone to over confidence or a lack of confidence, corruption, anti-social behaviour, and illusions about money.

My meagre knowledge of history is concentrated on industrial and maritime life from the middle of the nineteenth century but it's sufficient to produce ample evidence of greed causing suffering. We can read reports of the 19th century Royal Commissions into the plight of child chimney sweeps and match-factory girls with 'phossy-jaw'. Most people are aware of the overloading which created 'coffin ships' until 1894 when, thankfully, the Merchant Shipping Act made Plimsoll Lines compulsory. Less well known and considered are the remnants of inadequately regulated disregard of safety, greed by another name, which cost the loss of three Hull trawlers and many lives as recently as 1968.

Regulation is essential. Otherwise wealth soon converges on the individuals who have already acquired a comfortable excess of income or return on capital over their survival-needs: they can take risks. Any businesses that have become Big Business may be able to afford to trade at a loss in the short term to force out smaller firms and become Even Bigger Businesses. And, worst of all, wealth may converge on the unscrupulous who only wish to maximise their profits regardless of the consequences for others, sometimes misinterpreting Darwin's words as justification. So no support from me for those who call for deregulation because 'the market will sort everything out'. Ask the survivors of Bhopal!

Markets present problems: For those who actually do the farming, run production lines, trade across the seas, markets do not work quickly and they rarely produce stability. Does that matter? Of course it does. For instance, farmers compete in the market for their produce. They must decide between milk and meat, wheat for bread or barley for beer, chickens for eggs or turkeys for Christmas, or whether to scrap the lot and grow rape. Thus there is no guarantee that market competition will ensure that the nation is always well fed. In some places a lust for agricultural substitutes for hydrocarbon fuels already threatens food production, and there is ample evidence that dairy farmers are suffering because of the 'producers versus the supermarkets' system. Strategic changes take time.

Those we may call 'marketeers' work to a time scale several orders of magnitude faster. If farmers own their land they can make decisions in their own time and then stand or fall by them. But when farms become 'agribusiness' (which may in turn be part of some larger business) investors in the company's shares clearly prefer short term profits. Today's computers facilitate this to the nth degree: shares can be bought and sold in fractions of seconds: prices can be manipulated. That world belongs to the financial wizards. Some become obscenely rich. The people who actually work remain less well off. That's a problem we really should address.

Another problem occurs even when those financial wizards are using the money of those who wish to gamble. A 'Let's see who blinks first' boldness inflates market values beyond regions justified by the rewards which can reasonably be expected 'when the ship comes in'. Success therefore depends on selling out before the bubble bursts. Failure to judge the right moment might not be too bad for those well insulated by their wealth! But their failure also affects those who thought they were investing wisely for their pensions.

Someone from another planet, examining the way our financial world works, might be forgiven for thinking that people were created to serve business, especially the Big variety. Evidence points that way, when for instance, owners or managers put pressure on workers to work ever harder, longer, for less pay – or lose their jobs if the business is transferred to another country.

In crisis situations people may be willing to work extremely hard for their companies without complaint because the need to do so is clear. For many years I watched the post-war reconstruction of West Germany and saw how, when the 'economic miracle' had been delivered, my German family and friends wanted more from life than merely creating profits for others. Observed at a greater distance, there appears to have been a similar pattern in Japan. Those responses seem entirely appropriate to me: companies should exist to serve the community, not the reverse.

If not only profits, then what? How should companies serve the community? In the 1970s, Bernard Dixon, as Director of the then-named Institute of Personnel Management, was the first I heard suggesting that companies should recognise four responsibilities: to their shareholders of course, but also to their work force, the community in which they operate, and the environment. Thankfully similar ideas are now becoming slightly more common. Companies may profess Social Responsibility: whether they believe in it may be questionable in some cases. Do the banks come to mind?

An example of Social Responsibility in action would be supermarkets ceasing to use milk as a 'loss-leader' to attract customers. This would ease pressures which, even if unintended, are driving some dairy farmers off the land. And at the policy level, manufacturing, despoiled for years by a policy of preference for 'services', should be encouraged because it can be a vital contributor to keeping money circulating in UK instead of flowing out to pay for imports. And if there are still any companies that think it acceptable to rely on immigrants to provide cheaper labour, we should leave them in no doubt that that is not what business in Britain is for.

How can we control big business and the markets so that they work for the long term good of the community? Not easily I'm afraid. Markets can be and are manipulated - the housing market is an example which is discussed in more detail later. So what is to be done?

Internally, Government regulation must create a 'level playing field' for competitors in a market, force out gambling with derivatives and the like when the savings of others are involved, prevent big businesses becoming monopolies, and where necessary promote adherence to far-sighted strategies. If that sounds like socialism, I'm happy to be termed a 'little-s socialist'.

In the long term, as eminent economist Richard Picketty has suggested, international agreement is the way to combat the threat to democratic societies posed by ruthless capitalism. The first step towards that, he suggests, should be regional agreement through a degree of European political integration: anathema to some Brits. However, a step before that, I suggest, is that the British public learns to be angrier and to express that anger more effectively through the media. That's one of the outcomes I hope for after the people experience the shock of becoming the most senior kind of citizen in the land.

An example of righteous anger in action. My colleague at the Australian Bureau of Mineral Resources, the Chief Petroleum Engineer, was angry that the Woodside Petroleum Company intended to use an extraction technology which provided quick profits but left much of the oil in each reservoir in the ground, irretrievable. Normal government channels failed to act on the matter so he presented a paper publicly exposing the problem and suggesting an extraction technology which, in the long term, would double the yield of the company's rape and pillage method. I witnessed at close quarters the company response: Chairman and MD to our Director's boss, the Minister for Primary Industry and Energy; complaint to the Institution of Engineers Australia, etc. They prevailed! Some you win, some you lose. But it's right to try.

What about those other problems: jobs, welfare and pensions? The agricultural, industrial and information revolutions all reduced the number of people required to work. To maximise profits, a few kept their jobs and the remainder became unemployed. This provided a pool of cheap labour for industry and created problems in the areas of inequality, welfare costs and pensions. Unions were formed, then the Labour Party, both existing, initially at least, to establish and conserve conditions for those in work, rather than any wider considerations of the common good.

Despite the many benefits of technology, automation etc, workers are still essential to the production of goods and services and many would say they are being pressed to work harder and longer. However, the option of sharing the work to meet modest needs equitably among all the available labour force does not seem to have ever been considered very seriously. Instead, 'growth' to meet materialistic 'wants' stimulated by sophisticated marketing has been the suggested answer.

Personally I have always thought 'growth' to have a lot in common with pyramid selling, but that was not a popular view. And having never read John Stuart Mill's works, I was unaware that he recognised the wisdom of aspiring to a 'steady state economy' long before 'sustainability' took on its current meaning. Fortunately, the global imperative to consume earth's resources more prudently – or else! - seems likely to stimulate more enlightened thinking on the subject. Better late than never.

It is time to consider dumping the creation of more and more 'wants' and concentrate on 'needs'. There's no need to be too puritanical about reasonable needs, but, seriously, 'Who needs a £2,500 handbag'? That bag has been my favourite symbol of 'over the top' affluence, but as I update this text the Times records that the obscenely rich are offered handbags starting at £50,000, an offer declined by one lady who wouldn't spend more than £13,000 on a bag. How do they sleep at night?

Going back to needs rather than wants: those needs should be met by sharing the available work, at high and low skills levels, more equitably. When robotics take over many tasks, we should sit back and let them get on with it. And we should consider any new ideas which promote the wellbeing of society.

To give just one example of a new approach: in the autumn 2010 edition of the Permaculture journal, Chris Smaje explored how farms might look in a post-oil future. He describes a method of small-scale agriculture which, research suggests, if applied nationally, could produce all the food we need. The condition for that great achievement would be a larger number of people working on the land.

There must be many more novel ideas 'out there'. Would they not provide a fulfilling outlet for many poor devils who currently lack any employment if only we could all achieve a different work-life balance by revising our expectations, needs and what we 'must-have'?

Housing

Winston Churchill and Harold Macmillan both lived at a fairly high level of affluence, somewhat remote from the common herd, but to their credit they knew very well that everyone deserved a comfortable home, be it a house or a flat. They did not wish to repeat the post World War 1 disgrace of the government promising 'Homes for Heroes' which they failed to deliver. So in the 1950s Churchill's government worked hard to get homes built: Macmillan got industry to deliver 300,000 in the peak year.

Since then, population growth, inadequate government pressure to build affordable new homes, the 'right to buy' council houses, limitations on replacing council houses, and other factors, have created shortages leading to massive rises in house prices: scandalous from the point of view of those needing a home. Worse, a tendency to expect that house prices will always rise was created: an expectation recently proved false.

Many people now regard the market value of their homes as part of their 'pension pot' and in recent years some have benefitted greatly by the rapid rises consequent on the shortage of housing. However, even if abundant housing resulted in house prices becoming stable over decades, homes could still form part of people's pension plans. A 'starter' house or flat might be followed by a 'family' home and later by 'down-sizing' during retirement, releasing capital for other purposes. There is no excuse there for keeping prices artificially high by manipulation of supply. Nor should land be an issue: see Estates and Land later.

At present, it is commonplace to see that developers are merely required to build a token number of 'affordables' as a condition for a permit to build the more profitable category often known as 'executive' homes.   Would it not be far better to enforce the building of lots of affordable houses and flats as cheaply as reasonable standards allow? If that resulted in rich owners of properties losing rental income, so be it.

Is enforce too strong a word?   How did Macmillan get industry to deliver what the people of the country needed?   I haven't discovered that: the record of his life fills eight hefty volumes so the answer should be in there somewhere.   However he did it, he showed that it could be done!   It should be done again.

Health

When the NHS began in 1948 my pay as Cadet in the Royal Navy was reduced from 17 shillings and 6 pence a week to 15 shillings to pay for it. However, knowing that in the hard times of the 1930s, working class parents found it hard to decide whether a child's illness was severe enough to justify paying a doctor's bill, or even just buying calamine lotion to soothe chickenpox spots, I knew that the NHS was worth paying for.

It still is.   But that's not to say that we should do exactly the same again if we had a fresh start.   For instance, in Britain, GPs waiting rooms are usually packed with patients waiting for a consultation lasting very few minutes. Australian experience suggests that when people have to make a contribution to costs, they don't run to the doctor with trivia. Consequently waiting rooms are less crowded, and a standard consultation is up to 25 minutes. Such a fundamental change to entrenched expectations would be very unpopular in the UK.

However, if the financial pressures become too great we may have to consider adopting a contributory principle. Most working families could make a contribution to general practice, just as they do to eye care and prescriptions, and a 'safety net' could be provided for those unable for good reasons to do so. The individual amounts might be small but there would be millions of them, restoring in part or whole, financial equilibrium. In return families would continue to receive the hospital operations and other treatments, which may cost thousands of pounds, completely 'free at the point of need'. That's a thought to have in reserve.

Our biggest dilemma at present is how to correct a fundamental error made when the NHS was introduced. 'Free at the point of need' healthcare is funded nationally. Social care was seen as something separate, somewhat of a poor relation perhaps, to be funded by local government. We now know what an error that was. Progress in medical expertise and measures such as 'same-day surgery' allow patients to spend less time being treated in acute hospitals (sometimes whole wards have been closed), provided of course that essential follow-up care is available at patients' homes or elsewhere.

There's the snag: facilities for care outside the acute system and in homes has not kept pace. Patients cannot be discharged from hospital until appropriate care is available: the resulting 'bed-blocking' has become a major problem. A radical solution would be significantly more funding for more social care but it seems unlikely that any government will be willing to raise taxation sufficiently.

Fortunately, a convergent process, in which social and medical care in the community are gradually merged, could offer an alternative at a lower cost. There seems little reason why care workers could not be trained to take temperatures, check that people have taken their medication and similar duties, in addition to the usual showering, dressing etc.. The professionally trained nurses would then be free to concentrate on more complex matters. That's what we should work on.

Healthcare can undoubtedly be considered a morass of conflicting elements: ever expanding medical knowledge; effective but increasingly costly medications; increasingly complex and expensive operations; increasing population; increasing obesity; increasing life expectancy; decreasing effectiveness of antibiotics; increasing exposure to new strains and viruses from overseas; new issues such as female genital mutilation; increasing litigiousness; the list goes on. And like walking through a real morass, our journey through this metaphoric one must be careful step after careful step, heeding the words of expert guides. No quick fixes here please. Politicians must resist the temptation to reorganise and reorganise and reorganise.

Privatisation of healthcare: friend or foe? Can it help? As a member of a team advising the Trust Board on patients' interests at the Nuffield Orthopaedic Centre, one of Britain's five specialist orthopaedic hospitals, I watched the development under the aegis of the NHS of an Independent Sector Treatment Centre at Banbury. We visited the ISTC and were impressed: no fancy architecture, just a modest reception area and operational areas to match. Nothing to object to, much to admire. Except: the ISTC contract was to take some of the load off the NOC by doing what we referred to as 'bog-standard' knee and hip replacements.

This gives us just one final practical thought to leave with the politicians and experts who must wrestle with the complexities of healthcare. The ISTC was not contracted to do training of young surgeons and theatre nurses, or research into better operations and prosthetics. Training and research still had to be done at the NOC and similar centres of expertise. And what do young surgeons need when they first begin to gain experience? Lots of bog-standard operations. At its worst, if allowed to do so, the private sector will 'cherry pick'. At its best, it offers us a model for no-frills practice. Just think carefully about all the implications before placing contracts!

There is evidence that our civil service is not very good at negotiating tough contracts. Is our education system still somewhat biased against science, technology and business?

Education

It seems quite easy to define a couple of principles on which a truly democratic country should organise education. We: *should allow everyone to achieve their potential.* And: *education should prepare children for adult life in society and in the workforce.* But then we contemplate the very wide range of children's cognitive abilities, and many difficulties appear.

Although we are not yet a truly democratic country, there are no longer 'servant' and 'labourer' classes whose education can be limited to an 'elementary' level. There should never have been education policy which condemned masses of working class people to a minimal education regardless of their intellectual potential. That class-based system not only wasted a significant portion of the nation's brain power but also allowed some privately educated young people of very modest ability to find employment way beyond their true potential.

As recently as my generation the 'Eleven plus' examination was the determining hurdle. Those of us who were successful occupied the limited number of Grammar and High School places. The rest started work at 14 and for most children that was it. A few who failed the 11 Plus achieved great things later but that was due to their talents, not the system. Even those of us who passed were speedily divided into A and B streams at High School.

The changes introduced after World War 2 were well intentioned steps in the right direction but, over 60 years later, the debate still rages. Stability has not been achieved. Despite widespread public apathy and disbelief in religion, church schools still do not wholeheartedly recognise our social-animal nature. Anglicans, for instance, though having given up (as far as I can tell) the verse 'The rich man in his castle' continue to teach 'All things Bright and Beautiful'. Other faiths sometimes teach much less innocent doctrines.

Despite the raising of the school leaving age in England in 1997 to 18, the age of legal majority, there is evidence of young adults lacking the maturity to take on the responsibilities of adult life. Employers complain that too many candidates are ill equipped for the jobs they seek. And there is without doubt still a residual and unwholesome prejudice in favour of Grammar Schools and modern equivalents over Technical Colleges, and a tradition that values the classics and PPE over engineering and technology. Prejudice and tradition should be discouraged.

I must leave the search for better educational practice to the experts but believe we should work on one more principle: *our education system should allow those who are talented but 'late starters' to re-enter education and training at any age'.* And I have some suggestions at the practical level which follow from it, based on experience on advisory panels at the interface of engineering and education in Australia.

First we should close the deep social divide created by the UK's adoption of the devisive expressions 'Higher' and 'Further' education. That division prompted so many Colleges of Technical and Further Education to want to become universities and has eroded respect for the tradesmen and women, technicians and paraprofessionals without whose skills everyday life could not be sustained and high level research supported. Instead of Higher and Further we should define the spectrum of education as Primary, Secondary and Tertiary. At the emotional level, that simple spectrum of education minimises the temptation for university graduates arrogantly to feel that they are far superior to the students at the variously named Colleges which have succeeded the TAFEs. They may be more intellectual but they should respect the wide range of skills that others bring.

Fostering mutual respect between all tertiary education institutions may also reveal practical benefits. One university in Canberra (there were elements of four!) was surprised to learn that the Canberra Institute of Technology (ex-Canberra College of TAFE) had better facilities for some segments of first year engineering education: sharing was possible and capital investment could be conserved.

Much more importantly, collaboration at tertiary level encouraged articulation of the courses for technicians with four year engineering degree courses. This made it easier for any 'Techos' who had the ability and aspiration to become professional engineers to achieve their dream. Their 2 year 'full time equivalent' study for Certificates and Diplomas exempted suitable 'late starters' from the first year of the degree course. Good for them, good for the country.

A final bit of food for thought in UK. The conversion of so many TAFEs to universities has created a skills gap and now we need to attract people to learn increasingly complex trade skills. Some potential applicants may be 30, 40 or 50 years old. Now who, wishing to change direction at thirty or forty something, would wish to be called an apprentice?

Canberra was short of plumbers – isn't everyone? Offer a Traineeship, that's different. And not only for men. The idea attracted sufficient women plumbers to alleviate the shortage. Reserve the word 'apprentice' for teenagers!

Defence

Defence has one of the best known short titles, the MoD, and yet it may be the government department people know least about. Perhaps that's not surprising. In addition to the three armed services and the structures to administer and support them, the MoD works with 29 agencies. Quite a lot even for six ministers and six 'top brass' to manage. How much more difficult for outsiders to get to grips with it, especially as some information accessed through the website can only be described as turgid! Nevertheless it is possible to take stock of some aspects of defence.

The MoD faces the perennial problems of predicting what the next threat to the nation's security will be, procuring the weapons to counter the threat and the logistical support they need, and recruiting and training the required servicemen and women. Equipping the services, for example, has implications, not only for the fighting forces but also for industrial employment, arms sales profits and politicians' futures. Many of the complex difficulties are ably documented in Lewis Page's 'Lions Donkeys and

Dinosaurs', and Glyn Prysor's 'Citizen Sailors' records some of the consequences, human and tactical, of getting it wrong 'when it matters'.

We can look at the armed services which are after all the MoD's raison d'etre. From one angle they are still organised on traditional lines: a sense of personal connection between the Sovereign and the navy, a mishmash of territorial and modern army units, and a recently formed, historically speaking, air force. The services include some very different kinds of animals, as our Canadian colleagues found out when they tried to homogenise their three services. Our traditional approach has some silly and some quite strange features and at least one serious shortcoming. Is it not strange that air force officers carry swords like medieval knights, and the taxpayer is paying for an army unit, albeit a small one, which never goes to war?

More seriously: at the top there is a Chief of the Defence Staff, presiding over the competing heads of the three Services, each of whom has the right of direct access to the Prime Minister. That right and the usual empire-building and turf-protection instincts common to organic entities tends to promote inter-Service rivalry at the top level which sometimes does not serve the national interest well. For example, some Falklands veterans criticise the RAF's insistence of mounting an air raid on the Port Stanley airfield. It was not only immensely expensive in resources but, they suggest, counter productive and damaging.

There is no doubt that organising and conducting Britain's Defence is not an easy task and that consequently the MoD, like the NHS, is almost always undergoing change, especially in procurement. Given the historic background and the complexity, what significant changes would I dare to propose?

First, legislate for a Chief of Defence, appointed on a 'best person for the job' basis to command all three services. Cancel the right of direct access by single services to the PM: if individual service chiefs really cannot accept the position taken by the head honcho they can always resort to the time honoured option of resignation. Doubtless there would be immense anguish at first but after a few heads had been knocked together and a few years had passed a new generation of joint service thinkers would wonder what all the fuss had been about.

Cancel Trident. Despite the recent appearance of Russian aircraft on the fringes of British airspace, the threat of a 'conventional' nuclear war – a term unthinkable a few decades ago - is now sufficiently low that the Trident replacement programme could be abandoned. This would release funds aplenty to contribute to solving other problems, especially countering emerging threats, some of which may be more immediately threatening to British people on their own land.

It is worth remembering that our adoption of the earlier Polaris missile project did not give us a truly independent nuclear deterrent: the missiles were designed and made in the US. Furthermore, my recollection of the politics of the Nassau Agreement is that when Britain agreed to fund four SSBN submarines equipped with Polaris missiles, the US were reported to have cut their programme from 45 submarines to 41. Official confirmation of that particular bit of defence history would probably be impossible to find! No matter: in present circumstances cancelling Trident is a risk worth taking.

We must get to grips with the fancy dress brigade and those who think that the British services have a monopoly of smart ceremonial. Fortunately those for whom the services were a Gentlemen's club have almost completely gone. Lord Louis can't have been thinking very clearly when he suggested the reintroduction of polo into Malta only six years before the final exit of the British services in 1979. And although the young James (later Jan) Morris enjoyed the 'indulgent elegance of the 9th Lancers', he recognised that, to their credit, they had adapted to their modern, motorised cavalry role.

A bit of pageantry down the Mall is all very well but let us not overdo it. Let us be smartly uniformed, perfectly drilled to move as one, but let us leave the chain mail, breast plates and spurs behind. Parliamentarians should like this because good political points can be scored by telling the taxpayers how much money has been saved.

Moving on. Procurement is especially difficult when new technologies are being developed. The torpedo problems recorded in the book about Captain Dan Conley's 'Cold War Command' are a good example with which I'm very familiar. It is impossible to specify in contracts exactly how to deal with 'unknowns' which pop up. A *culture* of dependable mutual trust and confidence between selected contractors and the MoD would be wonderful if it could be achieved: pigs might fly. Alternatively, the government could create and engage with a single contractor called BAE in which it has a 'Golden Share' to give it total control over the company. Ever picked up the paper and read of retribution for BAE's shortcomings? The government should not be afraid to exercise its powers: our services and our taxpayers deserve no less.

Should the armed services ever be used against British citizens in 'Aid to Civil Power'? Precedent says so: Churchill was quite keen on it. Australian history, following that precedent, records some actions we would now consider shameful and until recently I would have thought it virtually impossible to imagine today's Aussie soldiers firing upon fellow citizens. However, both countries are facing new threats from within and an open mind is appropriate. But let us insist that our governments do not choose military action lightly.

Finally, when I read an appeal in the Oxford Times for four million Pounds to build a Soldiers of Oxfordshire Museum I responded with a letter. In it I suggested that though a museum might be a good cause, a better one would be to use any available funds to help meet the increasing needs of ex-service men and women, amputees, wheelchair-users and others. The museum was built and I have made my reservations known.

The care of veterans, especially those damaged mentally or physically in the service of their country is a MoD responsibility. There is an MoD agency devoted to their affairs but little evidence that it has sufficient clout. In the great world of Defence, could Veterans Affairs attract and retain the best people? In Australia, as in the USA, a Department of Veterans Affairs quite separate from Defence looks after veterans and their dependents in exemplary fashion. How come? One might say that those who work there are 'a different kind of animal'. Let us instead have a Ministry of Veterans Affairs with a small staff who are devoted to (and whose careers depend on success in) looking after our veterans.

The Policy and Practice Jigsaw
- more pieces

Having considered some major matters, I'm adopting an alphabetical listing for others.

Abortion. Even those of us with no close exposure to abortion cannot help being aware of the high prices to be paid for it, always emotionally, often morally, sometimes physically and financially. But if there is one thing worse than abortion it is the life of an unwanted, uncared for, or unloved child: better never to have been born. So: support for Choice.

Accountability, rights and responsibility. To supplement an ageing memory I keep a Scandal Sheet, based on news reports in the papers, on the television, radio and the internet, listing failures in public affairs in the UK. A common feature of many entries is the lamentable plea by politicians, officials, managers and the like that they didn't know that such illegal, immoral, inappropriate, dishonest, antisocial, indiscrete activities were going on. What I would like to hear or read more often is a plain reminder that people in positions of authority are 'Knaves if they knew and fools if they didn't'.

To put it in a practical employment setting: each charge hand, foreman, manager, director, chief executive and chairman of the board should be responsible for monitoring the behaviour and effectiveness of their subordinates and for keeping their superiors informed of problems. It can and should be as simple as that. At any level turning a blind eye or ear to something improper may be a temping option but if it is exposed, ignorance should never be accepted as an excuse. The buck stops somewhere: we must make sure we know where.

Moving on to personal aspects. We hear so much talk of rights! There seems to me to be only one natural right. In the words of the King James Bible, Genesis 3.19, 'In the sweat of thy face shalt thou eat bread until thou return unto the ground'. Or in blunt modern terms nature says, 'Work for your living or starve'. All other rights and benefits are bestowed by the community and could therefore be withdrawn by the community. And if abused they should be!

There seem to be murmurs that we are beginning, quite rightly, to remind young people of responsibilities neglected for several decades. I believe one deserves special emphasis. It is the responsibility of young men who show a conspicuous lack of awareness and acceptance that if despite modern birth control conception occurs, it brings responsibilities to contribute to the maintenance of the offspring until they are at least eighteen years old – the offspring, not the young fathers! It is a good place to start, provided of course that our enforcement is fit for purpose.

Advertising. They didn't bother advertising to young people in the early post-war years: we had little money to spend. Then what happened? Affluence. Now advertising creates demand, peers may jeer if some young person does not have the right labels on their clothes and shoes, the right accessories and the latest gadgets. Similar pressures are applied to adults. There is no doubt that the advertising industry is a prime candidate for opprobrium. Fortunately it is responsive to the amount of spending money available so if alternative work practices – see later - and higher priorities reduce the discretionary expenditure in certain areas the pressure should wither on the vine.

Age discrimination. I was 55 when I decided that I really must say goodbye to Defence and get a 'civvy' job and I'm pleased to record that it wasn't difficult – in Australia! The UK Equality Act of 2010 should have made it equally easy here but complaints are heard in news interviews and elsewhere that even 40-somethings are afraid they will find it almost impossible. So it seems to be a cultural problem not a legal one. Experience suggests that there is a fairly natural tendency for young 'bosses' to be disinclined to recruit older, more experienced subordinates who just happen to have been made redundant through a take-over or similar reason. We must support older candidates in such cases: fairness should trump prejudice.

Amnesties. Most Brits seem to like the idea of taking some firearms out of circulation occasionally without penalising the people handing them in, but when HMRC applied the principle to tax avoiders exposed by an HSBC whistle-blower, most interviewees wished for more prosecutions. Personal opinions or following a media line? Does it matter? Amnesties seem a useful tool for society if used sparingly even though liable to opposition if applied to new topics.

Adversaries. Much of the 'British way of life' since the Industrial Revolution has been based on antagonism: workers and bosses; unions and management; party politics; the judicial system; private and state schools. And there is often a tendency to believe that whatever we do in Britain is the 'right' way of doing things and to denigrate the ideas of others. One small but symbolic example was the criticism by some English commentators of the adoption of a semicircular layout for the Scottish Parliament's chamber.

Whether such attitudes are related to the class system or are a relic of Empire, or a bit both, is a question for academics. As people looking to the future we should open our minds to the ideas of countries which have impressive records of egalitarian wellbeing: the Scandinavian countries come to mind, and, of course, Canada, New Zealand and Australia. There will always be 'classes' with potential for separation by intelligence, wealth, power and influence but they will all prosper best if they are not at war with one another.

Arts. Given the many forms of art and the impossibility of achieving a single definition of artistic merit, continuing problems of selection and funding are inevitable. Kipling tells us that Ung, the maker of pictures and carvings, was cherished by his tribe: but not whether there was competition between Ung and the teller of tribal tales and singer of songs.

Aeons later but before installation art became prevalent, during a debate on art at an evening sculpture workshop in London, our tutor the late Kerrie Trengove challenged us with, 'The trouble for amateurs is that you confuse art and beauty'. We amateurs all agreed that unless we could perceive some form of beauty in a work, it was not art to us.

Conclusion: controversy is likely to be eternal. So who to feed? In general, let national and local governments leave it to the tribe to organise funding for the arts: individuals can contribute by attendance or donation, businesses can offer sponsorship. Taxpayers would have nothing to complain about.

Assisted suicide. I'm definitely in favour, simply because it's what I would want in some circumstances. If I were afflicted with 'Locked-in' syndrome for example, the knowledge that I could take my leave whenever I wished would be a great comfort. Neither the possibility of misuse or undue pressure, nor any antithetical views of the religious should be allowed to prevent passage of the necessary, carefully worded, legislation.

Those who are religious may linger in pain if that is their wish. They must not decide how the rest of us should die. So will Britain please legislate to allow those who are suffering from incurable diseases and wish to die to be assisted to end their lives painlessly?

Big Society. The former Coalition government's Big Society concept was to provide a force to help keep concerns for people's lives high on the policy agenda so that they are not obscured by the vocal concerns of businesses. The Big Society Trust was funded with £600 million but the one thing I have been unable to find on relevant websites is a simple lead to 'Achievements'. If they are doing great works they are not getting the good publicity they deserve. If they are not …………

Cashless society. When will a British government state clearly that the country should aim to become a cashless society? Of course there will be some - including some of my friends – who deplore the idea. They should not be heeded.

The benefits to doing virtually all our financial business electronically are great: no cash or cheque books to carry about (or lose); a computer record that we really did pay that bill; minimisation of 'cash in hand' trading and the associated tax evasion; reduced risk of roof repair and similar scams extracting cheques from vulnerable older people; and more, including of course the significant cost of producing and circulating notes and coins. Experience elsewhere suggests that those advantages outweigh the possible disadvantages of hacking etc. So rather than do it by stealth, the government should show leadership.

And meanwhile as a first step, we should scrap copper coinage. Pence coins probably cost more than their face value to mint and must cost the nation millions of pounds in circulating them and accounting for them. The rules for rounding up and down after abolition can easily be expressed in legislation. Cheques and online transactions are unaffected. The cost to Australia was estimated to be a one-off inflation of about 2%: a price worth paying for significant annual savings. I wonder how much it costs to mint and circulate a one Pence coin?

Censorship. Of course we must defend freedom of expression, a free press, etc. But are there limits which society would be foolish to ignore? I believe so, having been influenced by some words of wisdom at a debate at the Institute of Contemporary Arts, chaired by the eminent film critic Dilys Powell, circa 1978. Academics present were prepared to argue at length on whether violence on film or television led to criminal violence. A senior Metropolitan police officer bypassed them, 'You academics can argue for or against causation all you like. Any copper can tell you that exposure to violence can trigger "copy-cat" violence in vulnerable individuals'. I can believe he was right. We should be careful how much freedom we allow.

Charity and charities. Here's a multi-faceted topic. Good moral gesture? Or leftover condescension from earlier times? Charity as little people giving to good causes or as tax exemptions for rich public schools? Big splash with hyped-up Red Nose Day or establish yet another new local charity in memory of a family member or friend? What to think?

It's clear that charity is an increasingly complex part of contemporary British life across many socio-economic levels. However experience at the street collection level in Australia suggested that although those of British or similar ethnicity were interested, for some other cultures, charity began at home and stayed there: it's not universal.

Normally, charity should not be allowed to become an excuse for governments to neglect their duty of care. However, it's impossible to argue, for instance, that a government funded Coast Guard Service could have been more dedicated and achieved more than the Royal National Lifeboat Institution. And in some cases, like overseas aid in emergencies, there may be good reasons why governments should fund rescue work on our behalf by charitable organisations. But however much the government does, there will always be scope to do more. So more charities.

Many thousands of British institutions are 'Registered Charities' and their motives are a mixed bunch. It's easy to accept evidence that major charities are often demonstrably better than state institutions at executing the business of charity at home or abroad and that's good. But there are also examples of charitable status which can only be classified as entrenching unearned privilege.

Then there is the likelihood that donations by certain businesses to overseas charities are nothing but a form of bribery to secure contracts – and perhaps fill a few pockets along the way.

The topic appears to be ripe for a major 21st century overhaul. Meanwhile, we must all do as we think fit.

Civil Service. To an emigrant returning to the UK in 2002 the UK the civil service appeared to be running the country with the prime objective of ensuring employment for as many civil servants as possible. Perhaps it has always done so. A trivial example: would any other country in this electronic age expect its drivers to have a licence comprising a photo-card and an A4 sheet called the Counterpart Driving Licence? Risible! And for a far more important example: why could the service not devise an efficient system to ensure that males who father children support them financially? There are many other examples large and small. Sir Humphrey's empires appear to be thriving, despite the cuts ordered by the coalition government..

And thriving tribally as well as in numbers. I had an opportunity to talk to the Director General of the Department of Energy and Climate Change and the senior members of his team who will be responsible for introducing Smart Meters into all UK homes by 2020. I asked his PA whether any of the team had a technical background. 'No, we're all policy people' was his answer. Intelligent and charming men, all of them, but might not the team have been stronger if a few of them were intelligent, charming and professional engineers?

Civil servants have been pampered. I've never heard how 60 became the retiring age for civil servants instead of the usual 65 and I don't care why. Equal hard work for all, say I.

Compensating reductions. I haven't heard this expression recently. That's surprising because it's an important concept when times are hard and money limited. But perhaps not surprising, because empire builders and turf-protectors are always with us.

For instance, our government proposes to transfer funds and powers from Whitehall to metropolitan authorities such as Greater Manchester. So far I have not heard of any proposals for corresponding reductions to civil servants in Whitehall. We should be alert and express our anger if we are asked to pay for new provincial empires and an unreformed Whitehall.

Competition, contracting out and co-operation. Capitalists trumpet the merits of competition and there is no doubt that it can sometimes promote efficiency in the pursuit of profit. They and conservative governments therefore tend to favour contracting out.

However, there is an obvious but rarely stated starting point for a discussion about the merits of their argument. If public service people who do not have to make a profit cannot compete with commercial operators who must, they should either be paid off and their work contracted out, or sacked and replaced by employees who can.

That is provided of course that the playing field is level. If allowed to 'cherry pick' the private sector will contract to do the easy and profitable, and leave the rest to the taxpayer. See the experience with an Independent Sector Treatment Centre (ISTC) in the Health Service section. Or ask Royal Mail! Or…….

And let civil servants responsible for contracting-out beware. My experience confirmed that the private sector can be quite unscrupulous when pricing work. A drilling company supplied cost estimates for some seismic survey work to a big-name consultancy for use in studies of out-sourcing. Perchance that drilling contractor was subsequently invited to tender for the same work in competition with my drilling crews. Much higher prices then appeared. They didn't get the contract. It was not the only case.

Civil servants responsible for contracting must become far more savvy. During the outbreaks of MRSA and C-difficile a few years ago, as part of my association with the Nuffield Orthopedic Centre, I wanted to compare the (very low!) NOC infection rates with those of an orthopaedic ISTC. I used the Freedom of Information Act but all I learned was that the ISTC was not obliged to reveal its rates because 'It's not in the contract'!

Attractive though competition may appear, in public service there is often greater merit in collaboration. Twice I experienced the consequences of two distinguished professors, when appointed to public office, mistakenly introducing the competition for funds which is customary in university research, into the Australian Defence Science and Technology Organisation in one case, and the Bureau of Mineral Resources in the other. In both it proved seriously counter productive, embarrassing for their organisations and difficult for them to correct!

Consultants. Cynics may say that in public life consultants are retained to save official and politicians from having to do their own dirty work. When the out-sourcing of my little engineering team was being considered, they came, they saw, they advised keeping the work in-house. 'That's what I advised months ago', I remarked, pointedly, to our Director. 'You just don't charge enough', was the cheerful comment of the leader of the consultants: I liked him and most of the consultants I had to work with.

Admiration for their competence was quite another matter: I objected successfully to the review of my engineering team being led by a consultant who had never managed one. Let those who commission consultants be very wary, especially when it is taxpayers' money they are spending.

Convergence. The term has three contemporary uses. The convergence of wealth has already been mentioned. The convergence of technologies is principally driven by commercial forces and only a watchful eye is needed to ensure a level playing field and correct any tendency to monopoly.

The growth area in convergence is its use to describe the diminution of the great gulfs between the average levels of wealth of the western world, with the USA as the extreme case, and the developing countries, with China leading the push.

The disparity spans earnings, housing, access to healthcare and a host of other measures. One of these is the use of fossil fuels, illustrated most vividly by the cartoon characters in Franny Armstrong's film 'The Age of Stupid', convergence being represented by shrinkage of the over-nourished American and growth of the diminutive Asian. Reconciling the forces at work within the prudent global warming timescale will be difficult. Let us hope we can encourage the 'big boys' to recognise the urgency of the problem.

Corruption. Corruption is usual. That is not what many of us were brought up to believe in the UK. There was a sort of general agreement that it should not exist and it is to Britain's credit that there was probably relatively little. However, when we venture abroad and see what's going on in the rest of the world we discover how common it is. And it has increased in the UK at many levels of society: most noticeably when members of parliament were discovered to be abusing their expenses system.

There's no doubt that we should eliminate corruption and we should be prepared to take extraordinary measures to eliminate it from public office. In Australia it was necessary to legislate to allow a Commissioner of Police to sack members of a state police service without revealing his reason and without appeal. It was worth it. Dealing forcefully with corruption is good policy, everywhere.

Culture. My edition of the COED offers four definitions. Crudely shortened they relate to: the Arts; group behaviour; biology of cells; and growing plants. I believe the second deserves a special place in thinking about public policy.

The reason? As a sound bite I suggest: 'It fills the gaps'. Gaps exist because it is impossible to write perfect laws, specifications, rules and similar prescriptions for our behaviour in the community, business and employment. A *culture* of general agreement that things will be done, or not done as the case may be, can save many trees from the paper mill.

A light hearted example. Ever since sticking plaster replaced bandages, hospital staff have used it to cover walls with notices. To prevent it happening on the pristine walls of a new hospital notices saying 'Don't stick notices on walls' could have been displayed on the neat and tidy notice boards provided. Would that have prevented plastering the walls? Probably not. A *'culture change'* is needed in such cases – more difficult to achieve than issuing a directive but with better long term results!

Importantly: Judges interpret the imperfect words of our laws. Their task can and should be eased by always including a preface stating what the intention of Parliament was.

Culture change is never easy but sometimes it must be attempted if we are to get the best out of our society.

Drugs. Every aspect of this topic is in flux. The NHS must wrestle with the problem of whether we can afford to prescribe new drugs which save lives or extend them for a few months, but which cost many tens of thousands of pounds to supply each individual. The developments which save could also bankrupt us.

It's principle versus pragmatism again. There are procedures for trying to find the 'least worst' solution and we should feel sympathy for those who must make the hard decisions. The only alternative would be to set up procedures for affordable and efficient referenda and let the public decide such difficult questions.

Then there are the problems of recreational drugs, principally the health and legality aspects. Both have major financial implications. Both have long histories of social impact. The present situation appears to be that scientific study which could underpin legal and economic reforms is finding it virtually impossible to gain acceptance by policy makers.

There are many interacting factors for this, including the deaths, addictions, risks to brain development, entrenched political and religious positions, public prejudice, commercial interests, and criminality ranging from vandalism to murderous cartels. Surely we would be wise to insist that when reforming policy, scientific study outweighs prejudice and vested interests?

We could begin on a small scale by introducing free needle exchanges for injecting addicts. My understanding is that experience has confirmed that the costs of modest shop-front clinics are significantly less than those of treating infected addicts. So I vote for pragmatism. And although there is sure to be a protest that this is condoning illegality, it should be ignored because, as in many such cases, five or ten years down the track no one will be able to remember what the fuss was about.

Electrical power. Our zest for using it presents many problems. If we can generate it reasonably cleanly we can power trains, cars and much else with controlled emissions and minimum contamination of the atmosphere. So generating and using it wisely is a good cause.

One fundamental problem is that even if we generate electricity we cannot store it on a massive scale using batteries, capacitors etc. However, I can't help wondering whether one way of storing energy has been given the consideration it deserves. It is the use of power which is surplus to the night-time load to pump water back up to reservoirs thus providing some potential energy to contribute to hydroelectric generation for peak daytime loads.

Of course there are lots of factors in the equation: how much surplus power do we have at night, how big would the transmission losses be, and many others. Nevertheless, when I read about the strenuous opposition to creating reservoirs I can't help wondering whether reservoir storage is discarded on political and NIMBYistic grounds rather than on the learned advice of the power engineers that the sums don't add up.

One thing is sure. We've got to use less, or make more, or both, or risk the lights going out or some other nasty consequences such as air pollution. Not happy thoughts.

Elites. If we confine our thoughts to intellectual elites rather than outmoded elitism by birthright, we should agree that our specially gifted individuals have certain attributes. They exist; they have the potential to be of greater usefulness to society than us ordinary mortals; and they sometimes have a tendency to become arrogant. We should counter the latter with all the means at our disposal. But we should be pleased that as individuals or groups, they exist.

Enforcement. When asked the key to maintaining good behaviour in schools a retired Director of Education with considerable wisdom replied, 'It depends on our responses to three questions in children's minds: "Who's the boss?", "What are the rules?" and "Will they be enforced?" They probably apply equally well to adults, especially young ones. At home or at work, adults usually know who is supposed to be 'the boss' and what the rules are. However there is sometimes a lack of rigour in the formation of the rules and enforcement of them in British public life.

For instance, 'Breath-testing' was introduced to save life and limb by keeping alcohol-affected drivers off the road but it seems to have been considered unsporting to allow police breath-testing units to set up unannounced tests outside drinking clubs. British indifference to speed limits is without doubt the best example of a lack of strict enforcement: the Aussie policeman hiding behind a bush with a 'radar-gun', backed by a rigorous system of collecting substantial fines would soon persuade most drivers to be sensible. And the young Aussie owners of lovingly built 'street cars' soon learned not to attempt wheelies in Canberra when we threatened to legislate to crush their cars for such offences.

Unfortunately there are examples in many other fields of activity. The answer to question three should always be 'Yes!' And given the will and adequate priority, enforcement is neither impossible nor impractical. We should be prepared to provide the funding to support it. Enforcement of the rules will usually be cheaper in the end than the consequences of 'free for all'. And the offenders who claim that some measures are just 'revenue raisers' will never have my sympathy.

Entrepreneurs. Like intellectual elites entrepreneurs are a minority with uncommon gifts. How they manage to see possibilities which others, sometimes nations, have missed is a great mystery. One man on a trip to China thought that the dust produced in chopstick factories could be used to make eco-friendly dog bowls and other products for pets. Was the co-founder of Beco Pets potty? Sales of over half a million bowls suggests far from it!

We should cherish our entrepreneurs, provided of course that they have the public good in mind as well as the rewards for their initiative.

Estate Agents. The sub-title 'and how they get away with it' of a book called 'The Establishment' could easily be applied to Estate Agents. It's nice to have some near the bottom of the 'status of occupations lists', but how do so many survive and flourish? Do we really need to feed so many?

It's beyond doubt that they have become accustomed to living very well indeed at our expense. A London agent took a young friend and me in his Porche people-mover to view a small house; there is a Property section of about 128 pages in the Oxford Times each week; and the number of agents' shop fronts in small market towns like Witney all testify to that.

Housing is arguably the greatest failure of public administration in Britain at present. We would be wise to scrutinise every factor which might make housing more expensive. Agents' fees might be one of them.

Estates and land. The only ducal estate I've observed for some years is Blenheim. My conclusion: given a good CEO and a well managed team the estate could survive the abolition of dukedoms without difficulty and would continue to be a source of great pleasure to its immensely varied visitors. Mr Marlborough's retention of modest quarters could doubtless be arranged at a suitable rent.

Most big estates are probably in a similar position: financed by safari parks, conference centres, etc. And if there are simply too many palaces and country houses, some will have to go. Tough but not a great problem.

One of the most remarkable books I've discovered recently, Who Owns Britain by Kevin Cahills, tells the fascinating story of the publication between 1874 and 76 of the four volumes of 'The Return of Landowners' which recorded ownership of all the land in Britain and Ireland. It also tells us of the subsequent political shenanigans, mainly in the Lords, which resulted in The Return disappearing from public view.

Most importantly Cahills tells us that 95% of the land in England, Scotland, Wales and Northern Ireland is still owned by about 37,000 people and institutions. The rest of us, 60 million or so, have to manage with 5%. The possible implications for land for housing and the rents of tenant farmers, reflected in the costs of our food, are uncertain but probably adverse. We should not shrink from mitigating this appalling imbalance by compulsory purchase when land is required for homes or other good causes.

Ethics. Not an everyday word for most of us. We may read about Ethics Committees examining new drugs but that's pretty remote stuff. However, sometimes ethics come much closer to everyday life. A senior civil engineer friend tells of his professional engineer team driving gritting trucks when the drivers were on strike. The drivers' union was incensed, until that is, my friend pointed out that the engineers were compelled to do so because the ethical code to which they were bound required them to place the public good, road safety in that case, above all other considerations.

In Australia I interviewed immigrants who were seeking recognition as professional engineers. Those from countries with dictatorial regimes found it really scary that they might have to contradict or refuse orders from superiors, politicians or others in authority in order to conform to our 'public good' ethical requirement,. And I sympathised: acting ethically may take courage but it has to be done. It is not just something for remote committees. Ethics should be more widely discussed.

Expectations. There is plenty of evidence that expectations form an important framework for happiness and unhappiness. Retiring to a new bungalow with, for the first time, a refrigerator and central heating gave my parents pleasure. Slowly acquiring electric toasters, television sets and similar devices was similarly pleasurable for my generation when we married. The reason: our expectations were being exceeded.

Contrast that with the unhappy single mother who complained in a television interview, that her state benefits were not enough to buy sufficient food. Conspicuously in view were a packet of 'Wetwipes': a welcome but expensive luxury in the eyes of pre-Wetwipe others, now seemingly a necessity commanding a higher priority than food.

The lesson of that bit of trivia? When and where necessary we must damp down expectations and not allow the advertising and marketing people to persuade people that they 'must have........'. Micawber revisited in a slightly different form I think.

Fairness. It has always fascinated me that children display a natural sense of fairness remarkably early in their lives, usually when they feel unfairly treated, and apparently without it being introduced by nurture. We need look no further to realise that fairness is one of the most important building blocks of civilised life.

It is also true that as a Daily Mirror headline put it four decades or so ago, "Life is not fair and systems cannot make it so". Nevertheless, whether we call it

'The Dunkirk Spirit' or 'Equal Misery for All', it is sensible for governments do all they can to mitigate the inherent unfairness of life.

The media also have a major role to play. In recent years, it has become common for pop stars or other media 'celebrities' to support particular good causes, perhaps a natural disaster or an attack on a child in some faraway country. A massive charitable campaign is launched and the near-hysteria mentioned earlier comes into play. There is scant regard for disasters and mayhem occurring elsewhere. Governments and media both have world wide contacts: it would be good to see them used to make our awareness, and our responses, as fair as possible.

Fear. Despite thousands of responses to the word fear on the web I haven't been able to find a simple scale for measuring fear: it may be impossible to devise one. However, we might assume that at one end of a scale would be the fear induced by a lunatic who has already killed many victims and who is pointing a gun at ones head at close range with the obvious intention of shooting any moment now. What's at the other end? Could it be the fear that in a democratic society a politician will not be re-elected if he or she has frightened the voters with unpalatable truths about the future?

Fear is probably the ultimate motivator. Perhaps the time has come when we could do with a little more of it to encourage us to face the challenge of climate change. Politicians please be brave, get the message across more clearly because that risk of inaction is infinitely more important than the risk to your career.

Feminism.   Worth a mention after all that has happened since 'The Female Eunuch'?   I think so, if only to pay tribute to the women who have talked practical good sense which seems to have muted the strident voices of yesterday.   My favourite example: one of the first professional civil engineers to work in the macho construction industry in Australia.   She agreed to wear a pink hard hat on site. Thus identified, men peeing in the trenches had time to up-zips before she walked by – a well mannered lot those Australian construction workers.

More importantly, I remember her predicting that the last right to be won by female engineers will be the right to be mediocre.   Fair comment: we can't all be brilliant, but the frontrunners had to be.

The basic problems remain: balancing career and childcare, equality in the highest ranks and boardrooms.   I would be very happy if any feminists find helpful the conclusion defined later

Happiness.   During a short course in economics at Bristol University about forty years ago a lecturer pointed out the weakness of Gross National Product as a measure of the wellbeing of the nation: what use would a massive GNP be if a significant part of it was the manufacture of Aspirin and the like to cure headaches induced by our lifestyle? I suspect that little more has been said on the subject in England until the recent recognition of the importance of happiness by the Coalition Government.

As recorded earlier, I believe most Aussies have a clearer perspective on their work/life balance than many Brits: you work hard during the week so you can enjoy your favourite recreation at the weekend. Whether we label it happiness or wellbeing, any effort to improve the balance in the UK should be welcomed. It is worthy of more academic study. Perhaps we should also take greater note of how Denmark appears to be the happiest country.

Health and Safety. OH&S has been allowed to become a bit of a joke in Britain because, many argue with some justification, it has been taken to extremes. In 1988 I spent six months studying the implications of new Australian OH&S legislation for the Bureau of Mineral Resources and drafting a manual of policy and practice. The boxes were ticked and a starry award received but the management did not endorse the policies in the manual and they never published it. After I left the BMR I heard that someone had been killed during off-road fieldwork because there was not a steel-mesh barrier between the load compartment and the seating of the 4 x 4.

We should be prepared to take OH&S very seriously. A few months ago the driver of a van was killed in an accident on the A40. The heart attack which caused the crash was not his. It happened to a man driving on the opposite side and his car veered across causing a head-on collision with the van. We shall never know whether the van driver would have survived if the chest freezer in the back of his van had been behind a strong barrier! My letter drawing attention to this sad thought was not published. OH&S is not a subject for joking

Hostage ransoms. The 'no ransom payments' policy of the British and US governments is not keeping hostages alive though it is denying ransom funds to the captors. The latter might be a significant factor in opposing fanatics such as the Islamic State terrorists. But is the policy deterring people, be they yacht owners, idealists or zealots, from placing themselves in harms way? It seems not. Is the policy a contribution to an international effort? No, some nations pay the ransoms and their people usually live.

So why not have a case by case policy? At least that would give the captors a motive to keep hostages alive in the hope of ransom. And such sums as might be paid would not seriously impair funding action against enemies such as the Islamic State after the hostages are safely home – or would that be unsporting?.

Hysteria. I can't escape the feeling that the behaviour of British people coming together as mourners, audiences etc verges on hysteria. That's bad enough when it is obviously whipped up by an off-screen studio manager waving a board calling for 'Applause and Whistles'. But there are circumstances when people have a clear choice and yet still behave like automata. A cause for concern?

It has been suggested by a family member, born post WW2, that hysteria is neither just a British characteristic nor a modern phenomenon. Nevertheless I have witnessed changes in British behaviour from the austere 'thirties and 'forties (excluding VE and VJ nights!) which coincided with increasing affluence. Up to a point the changes were for the better. The stiff upper lip was exchanged for a willingness to exchange hugs. However, we seem to have leaned more and more towards public demonstrations of emotion, especially, but not solely, in relation to deaths.

Are the media encouraging these superficial expressions of emotion? Have hysterics almost become obligatory in some circumstances? Are they distracting some of us from serious thought? I fear it might be so: the tendency should be discouraged.

Immigration. So much has already been said. From an economic point of view I agree with the suggestion that the UK adopts a 'points system' for immigrants from outside the European Union so that we only get immigrants who really will be useful to the country one way or another. I speak with experience. When I emigrated to Australia in 1979, I was appointed to a job which officers in the Royal Australian Navy didn't want because it was with the Science and Technology Organisation, out of the promotion mainstream.

However, the economic view doesn't help us decide what to do about the thousands of would-be-immigrants already attempting to migrate by fair means or foul to more northerly climes like Britain. Public reaction is already divided: if we decide they are *refugees* – see later - they may be received warmly by some even if rejected by others. If *immigrants,* opinions would often be less benevolent.

Immigrants and refugees pose problems by the pressures they place on the resources of our small country. But whatever we call the people coming from Africa and elsewhere in tens of thousands now, they are likely to be numbered in millions during coming years.

Britain is likely to remain a popular destination but it will be quite impractical to accept many into the UK. We shall have enough trouble dealing with our own population growth, discussed later. So I fear we shall have to take a strong stand against any mass migration. And starting now may be the best policy.

I'll just add one more thought: any immigration system is only as good as the enforcement of any conditions which may be attached.

Inheritance. This is undoubtedly a key to maintaining the country's fine old class system. As recorded in Land and Estates above a few thousand people 'own' 95% of the land. I haven't found a corresponding dramatic figure for unearned wealth. And I have to concede that the expression 'the idle rich' has fallen into disuse during my lifetime. Nevertheless, inheritance of land and wealth on a grand scale obviously still occurs.

The old term Death Duties has been replaced by Inheritance Tax, but there is a difference. Reading suggests that Death Duties were dreaded and loathed by the well to do. That was not surprising when so many estates had to be surrendered in payment of the death duty, among them one for which I have great affection: it is now the Westonbirt Arboretum.

Now Inheritance Tax affects middle managers and the like while the rich and landed go sailing on with trusts protecting them generation after generation: I haven't discovered any evidence that Inheritance Tax was paid on Blenheim.

There is talk that by the time this is published the tax threshold may be raised to £1m. I hope it is, but I would also like to see a radical rethinking of inheritance based on the principle that each generation must start from a modest base.

Law and Order. Crime rates have been reported to be falling all around the world and some politicians have been quick to claim the credit for this. However there are still plenty of serious offences which must be dealt with by our experts: major frauds; organised crime; paedophilia; grooming and other sexual crimes.

Ordinary people are, I suggest, more concerned with the everyday disregard of law and order which now makes daily life miserable for many people in the UK: theft, housebreaking, stabbings, assault, hooliganism, drunkenness, graffiti, loud music and so forth. The wisdom of 'prevent misrule from starting' has been disregarded. Criminality at various levels is widespread and the police are, too often, 'Sorry, but no one is available'. It is not surprising that the old understanding that we are *governed by common consent* has been replaced by a distrust of authority. And that distrust has been increased by suspicion following the privatisation of some law and order functions. So what now?

The first food for thought is the principle on which our Armed Service discipline is usually founded, *'There is no such thing as an unimportant detail'*. It removes the necessity for those who are not very bright to discriminate between different levels of importance, and bright graduates at Sandhurst and the other officer training institutions are exposed to it in the interest of fairness. It usually works well for the Services.

A policing strategy similar to that was tried by the New York Police Department and others in the 1990s: zero-tolerance of petty crime and incivility. Skimming the evidence suggests that if the community, the police and the justice system worked together and actions were all well focussed and managed, tough policing may have done much good and certainly did no harm. The difficulty, as so often, was proving causality: did these things just happen at that time for entirely unconnected reasons?

An alternative was related by a British Chief Constable in a media interview several decades ago. Asked how he had stamped out the 'dead end kids' gang culture in his city he reported to have said something on the lines of, 'We made it unsafe for the bad guys to go out at night'. News reports suggest there would be quite a few policemen and women willing to enact rough justice if they were sure a blind eye would be turned. However, the dangers of saying 'Go get 'em' are well known, as are those of vigilantism. Sanctioned violence would be completely morally wrong of course. But supposing we allowed things to get so bad there was no alternative? See Principle and Pragmatism.

To make sure things do not become that bad we should ensure that we match expectations of behaviour within the law and enforcement. It will be expensive but it will be worth it. And we must ensure that it applies to everyone: I would not like to see security for the few by way of gated communities with armed guards, Los Angeles style, in Britain!

Liberty. Liberty as we understand it in western nations – liberty within the law - is certainly worth defending but like many other benefits of civilised life it can rarely be absolute. In this present time of terrorist threats some aspects of liberty may have to be curtailed for the common good: just as freedom to travel to the seaside was off limits when invasion was threatened during WW2. Such sacrifices as may be required should be accepted willingly – provided they are applied fairly.

A few days after the pragmatic line above was written, it was reported that Liberty and other organisations has told the Parliamentary Intelligence and Security Committee charged with oversight of the Government Communications Head Quarters that they opposed on principle any intrusion into the privacy of peoples communications, even if it resulted in some deaths from terrorist plots which might have been prevented by intrusion.

I was sorry to hear that. It would be naïve to believe that there will never be some 'dirty work' to be done to defend our liberty. The spectrum includes not only GCHQ and MI6 activities but also intelligence gathering submarine snooping, SAS intrusions to release hostages, etc. We must rely on the honesty of selected representatives to have oversight of them to ensure that they remain within limits acceptable to the majority of the people.

Manufacturing v service industries. Recent history can easily be summarised here. Prime Ministers Thatcher and Blair turned their backs on manufacturing, favouring service industries instead. Conventional economists looked kindly on that. Their views might be summarised as, 'The UK is the world leader in finance, cultural industries, design, some areas of consultancy, and retail. Leave making stuff to the Chinese'. Such views are usually associated with expectations of reasonable stability and growth. Despite some evidence that when 'times are hard' foreign owners are likely to shut down their overseas factories first, foreign ownership is not seen as a threat. Two comments seem appropriate.

First, I cannot understand why we no longer seem to recognise that activities which keep our wealth circulating within the country, rather than sending it overseas to pay for imports, are worth six to seven times their initial face value. This rule of thumb, I was taught, was based on banks keeping reserves of about 15% and the rest being available for reinvestment loans. It seems to me we would do better if any vast sums earned by the service industries could be spent or invested here in the UK on things we need - and perhaps a few things we want.

More importantly, we are not living in a time of stability. Nothing could be more obvious than the political instability in eastern Europe and the Middle East; climate change is already changing weather patterns and increasing the threat of more famines in Africa; scientific studies suggest that the next thirty or so years may be critical for life on the planet. Britain is not immune from various pressures from these sources. In such circumstances it is as well to be able to provide the essentials of life, food, shelter, etc, with as little reliance on overseas sources as possible.

Perhaps I'm too gloomy but my generation remembers the shortage of food during WW2 and how many thousands of seamen lost their lives bringing supplies to us.

Means testing. Many Brits are still haunted by the means testing of the 'thirties. In Australia means testing of income and assets is recognised as an important tool for targeting retirement pensions and welfare and health benefits fairly. For some purposes the test is simply 'does this person have to pay income tax?' More complex applications would be used to assess whether a person is eligible for the means tested retirement pension. In Britain tax returns could, for example, be used to assess eligibility for the winter fuel allowance. It only needs the tax data base to be efficient to make it work. Need I say more?

Multiculturalism: I'm sorry that this ill-defined concept has become unpopular in the UK. When I immigrated into Australia it immediately became clear that it is natural for newcomers to be met and welcomed by their own kind: in my case mostly expatriate ex-Royal Navy officers. Then my Pommie Australian circle gently expanded to overlap with those of the Armenian Australians, German Australians, Italian Australians, Tamil Australians, Hungarian Australians, and even some dinkum Aussies. And as the years went by I recognised how sport, intermarriages and other influences softened the cultural boundaries even further. That was the kind of multiculturalism I liked: a good kind.

I do not know to what extent recent world affairs, especially terrorism and religious sensitivities, have affected the present day Aussie ethos: I'm just not close enough any more. But I do know that there is still a clear concept of what it means to become an Aussie. The responsibilities of every Australian citizen are: to obey the laws of Australia; to defend Australia if required; to serve on a jury if called; to vote in Federal, State and Territory elections and Referenda.

The implications of those simple words are enormous. No such concept of what it means to be British has yet been so unequivocally stated. That's an omission we should rectify. A written Constitution is required and I'm pleased that the LSE's Institute of Public Affairs have opened discussions on possibilities.

Overseas Aid. At first sight this might appear to be another fragment of the residue of empire. The residents of some ex-colonial countries do appear to believe that Britain owes them support. And perhaps, sometimes, they are right. Even major dominions like Australia were seen as a source of raw materials for British mills: building factories locally was not encouraged. And Britain is not the only country with this history: interactions between France and her former colonies sometimes followed similar lines. However, times have changed, fresh thinking is appropriate.

There are signs of international recognition that developing countries should be helped. Why? Probably for mixed motives: governments because aid might bring useful political influence in the recipient country and international Brownie points for being the good guys; businesses for the obvious reason, profit; and the altruism of humanitarian organisations. And railing against these views we read of the opposition of the 'Times are hard: charity begins at home' brigade. What to think?

First, we should not offer aid simply because Britain was once a colonial power. Many former colonies were left in reasonable order, some have thrived, some have disappointed. Others, from which we departed in haste, India, Pakistan – later divided to create Bangladesh, have had mixed fortunes for complex reasons.

After that it seems a matter of do we want to take a hard or soft line?   Probably sometimes one thing, sometimes the other.   A rigorous, unsentimental examination on a case by case and Budget by Budget basis should follow, always remembering that the government should be acting on behalf of the British taxpayer whose money it is.

And our officials should remember that a Budget commitment to dedicate a certain percentage of GDP to Overseas Aid is merely stating a maximum, not an obligation necessarily to expend it.

Population growth.   It's amazing that so large an elephant can occupy a corner of the room and not be overwhelmingly conspicuous. A recent report tells us that Britain's population is growing by 400,000 each year. Despite, or perhaps because of, the implications of that figure, the government has chosen not to risk increasing public awareness of the problem and the consequences of possible solutions for housing, feeding and finding work for them all.

Doubtless that's because any solution will arouse fierce local objections.   Most of us feel that it is a crowded world and that our Britain is more crowded than most. And opinions tend to be particularly strong when we read too that many people fiercely oppose the building of more homes 'in their backyard'.

And we may think there is another elephant in the room: 'don't mention birth control'. The Chinese one child policy 'has been a bad experience: there won't be enough young people to care for the old.'

It is pretty obvious that we must rely on experts at the UN and elsewhere to study the international aspects of the problem, especially mass migration. We should applaud the efforts of all who are working on the population problem. But whatever the outcome in terms of magnitude and timescale, humankind will have the usual choice: selfish self-preservation or altruistic cooperation for a common good.

Government and people should do what we can to prevent water-wars, food-wars and benign-territory wars becoming humankind's way of dealing with the problem. And bless contraception!

All we can do is insist that our government keeps us informed. For our part we should resolve not to shoot the messenger, even if the government's news is not to our liking. And we can be pleased that not all the news is going to be bad. Our descendents may, if UN scenarios quoted by economists like Thomas Picketty become reality, experience a peak in population around 2050 followed by a decline.

So much for the highest level thinking. Closer to home I was cheered to read Janice Turner's article in the Times of 31st January 2015 which followed a conference of the recently formed lobby group Ageing Without Children. She reminded us that although some youthful energy will always be needed to help frail older people, there are various ways in which people might mitigate the effects of an imbalance between the old and the young.

Principle and pragmatism. It would be lovely to be purely a man of principle. Principles are fine but they can lead to extreme measures. What if, in a position of authority, one might have to commit others to die for one's principles? What will historians conclude about the Falklands war years hence? Was the war justified as an act of principle? And if so, would the justification withstand scrutiny if the population of the islands were 100, 10 or 1? Principle moderated by pragmatism seems the best guide in virtually every case.

Prison. I've been in a prison several times but only at the request of the Governor of Portland Prison as part of an Admiralty Underwater Weapons Establishment's chess team: interesting but not much help on this topic. Nor was being invited to break into the army's Hilsea Barracks to test their security. The soldiers captured us but were poor jailors, failing to remove matches from my pockets which allowed me to set fire to the mattress in my cell during my brief imprisonment.

However, one experience did teach me how being a prisoner can change people in a matter of hours. Although not an airman I took part in an 'escape and evasion' exercise for aircrew who might be shot down. About a dozen 'crews' of three were dumped from a blacked out bus in the middle of a winter night in wildest Scotland; the known safe-house tens of miles away; 1,000 soldiers and police on the lookout for us; professional interrogators ready for anyone captured. And, unwilling to swim icy waters, captured most of us were. We were crammed into a single cell with only standing room and left for a few hours. Our mood changed in those hours and when our 'jailor', a fellow officer, was persuaded to open the cell door to allow a visit to the heads we simply trampled over him and returned to the hills – and I mean trampled!

The 20th century Royal Navy didn't have a prison. Instead it had Detention Quarters: high staff to offender ratio; high activity rate, offenders were always very fit at the end of a spell in DQ's; minimum talking between detainees, maximum sentence ninety days. Successful? If I remember correctly the re-offending rate was about a third of the civil prison rate.

The present day facility, the Military Corrective Training Centre at Colchester is reported to be producing similar results: 8% reoffending compared to the civil prisons 25%. There are complex reasons for the difference but as HM Inspector of Prisons suggested, the civil prisons could learn from the military. Worth considering.

Prostitution. The oldest profession is not going to go away: it's another of those 'constants of history'. So society has a choice: the street or the brothel. Anyone familiar with seaports will have seen both. I once spent a night in and out of various brothels in Oran – as Officer of the Naval Patrol, I hasten to add. Australia added to my experience: scantily dressed girls were still on the chilly pavements of Kings Cross, their pimps close by, at 5 AM as I left Sydney to drive back to Canberra,.

By contrast, in Canberra I witnessed the introduction of licensed brothels. They were situated in industrial areas, all run at that time by women, not a pimp in sight. Strict surveillance kept crime at bay. We heard of the gratitude of some handicapped men for the attentions of some kindly prostitutes. And, as our Capital Territory Chief Minister noted after she visited one of the brothels, there's another advantage, 'They pay their income tax'.

I would legalise brothels tomorrow to get all prostitutes off the streets of Ipswich and everywhere else.

Racism. Just one thought to add to this hot topic. And it's not mine. Memory tells me that it was published in Father Trevor Huddleston's book Naught for Your Comfort, published when Apartheid was threatening South Africa. He suggested that racism was a natural part of our primitive being and that it was the obligatory duty of Christians to rise above such instincts. I haven't been able to check my recollection. However, it still sounds like an accurate observation of human thought and behaviour and a good response, not only for Christians but for all men and women of goodwill.

Referenda. UK interest in referenda seems to be increasing. The Swiss use them quite often, why shouldn't we use them more? It should be one of the finest forms of democracy. There's a simple reason for caution. They can be too easily manipulated.

Reputable polls showed that 86% of Australians thought that the country should become a republic. The Prime Minister thought otherwise and by the time he had muddied the waters with publicity about the election of a future President, and chosen the words of the question accordingly, most voters felt they could only vote No. And the Australian record clearly indicates that No is the default choice. So use with care, beware of biased publicity, and keep questions simple.

Refugees. Most of us were appalled by the deaths of thousands of refugees drowned when the boats in which they were trafficked capsized or sank on passage to Italy. But how many of us even remember that over a million people may have died during the Ethiopian famine in the 1983/85? And what is the connection between those tragic events?

It is that most refugees are seeking to escape from persecution or other cruelty in times of war or civil instability, or from natural hazards such as drought causing famines, or destructive tsunamis. Or, worse and far too commonly, they flee from a combination of both kinds of threat.

Once again the principle is clear. We feel compassion for the tens of thousands of people who presently survive horrific circumstances and evil exploitation to seek new homes in European countries and expect our governments to find ways of sharing the responsibility for accommodating them.

However, it is the number of refugees that is the biggest threat. If - or is it when? - climate change intensifies the famines and political upheavals of, especially, Africa, and the starving, would-be refugees are counted in millions rather than tens of thousands, what then? Will pragmatism require us to pull up the drawbridge?

I suspect there wouldn't be any other answer. So unless we, the well-fed world, want to risk being faced with that possibility, we should sound the alert and send our ministers to the international conference tables to bring a greater intensity to seeking agreement on actions to avert such crises before they develop. The alert should be sounded now!

Research and development. This is another area in which Britain still seems to have a residual distaste for engineering and technology. Much brilliant work is done in those fields and in medicine, pharmaceuticals, instrumentation for space science, and others. But it tends to be done despite the nation's sub-optimal investment in R and D. How much better if we cut some of our more frivolous activities and matched the levels of leading nations?

Perhaps the most unusual discovery of recent years was the isolation in 2004 of graphene by two Russian-born researchers at Manchester University, work which earned them the Nobel Prize in 2010. The dates are important. British interests now own only 1% of the world patents. Where did the initiative go?

What can ordinary folk do to help? They can at least encourage those conducting R and D in their local areas by visiting 'open days' and drawing attention to the importance of their work in Letters to the Editor etc. Angry letters if good work is not getting the support it deserves!

Salaries. Obscene is a word to be used sparingly in almost any context but it's hard to believe that it isn't justified when some people are paid salaries and bonuses of millions of pounds a year when others get as little as £15,000. Controlling payments to business chiefs, stars of film and stage, footballers and celebrities in general is said to be impossible: 'we' sanction those payments one way or another, as shareholders, at the box office, at the turnstiles. However, 'we' could control the pay of our top Civil Servants, fixing it as a multiple of the lowest salary paid. At least that would encourage possible action in other areas.

Secrecy v openness. There were good reasons why in some of my navy appointments I travelled with a locked security briefcase. The reasons for a general cult of secrecy in public life in Britain are less obvious. The song about the Foreign Office with the advice, 'Never reveal your age or sex' was written many decades ago but media allegations of improper secrecy were made only a week ago, concerning the arming by stealth of many more policemen and women.

If the cause is good, secrecy may not do any harm. But it can be used to help officials and our representatives on councils and in parliaments get their own way against the wishes of the electorate. A campaign of public protest forced the Oxfordshire County Council to postpone their plan to favour urban libraries by closing rural ones, and they had to issue a consultation paper.

We expected a brief summary of the options with a few words on the advantages and disadvantages of each. No such luck: only the rural closures option was presented. My protest to the official responsible was met with, 'The law only requires me to present one'. We should not let our councillors employ officials with that kind of mentality. Despite opposition we found a way of keeping our highly valued village library open.

Whether matters are parochial or of national importance, openness is a fundamental component of democracy.

Slaughter. Back to religion again! Ritual slaughter has been a topic of discussion and some passion recently. When I accompanied a friend to a slaughterhouse in the Fareham area I was impressed by the killing of cattle. They appeared quite accustomed to entering the 'press': 'Been in lots of times for my injections and examinations by the vet'. The drop after the captive-bolt gun was instant and dramatic. Then, before they showed any sign of recovery from stunning, a cut and bleeding finished the job.

Then I asked about the contraption in the corner. It was the shechita frame in which in which cattle were turned upside down before their throats were cut, without stunning of course. I'm glad I didn't have to witness their distress.

I've only that brief experience of slaughter of cattle, none of sheep, pigs or chickens, nor of halal methods. But I'm certain that if I had to select a method for my own death by execution it would be the stun-gun and bleeding. Our national policy should be to insist that everyone conforms to the law of our land and our law should insist on the most humane methods.

Taxation.   Simple message: we should be prepared to pay for the sort of country we want. If that means that middle managers and others at similar levels have to pay a 50% tax on some of their earnings, so be it: provided of course that our taxation system collects even more from the much richer business barons, bankers and the like. I can vouch for the fact that it's worth it when the result is good living. Don't be a whinging Pom!

The United Nations.   Goes without saying: to be supported and encouraged to evolve unless someone finds a better system which we all agree to implement. Enough said.

Tobacco.   We are an odd lot. I don't think any British government would ever suggest we return to using asbestos as insulation in our roof spaces and elsewhere. Which of us would wish to risk developing the invariably fatal mesothelioma? And yet we allow our governments to fail to exterminate the tobacco companies which offer us a somewhat similar death from lung cancer and other diseases.

No holds barred I say.

Unions. Still needed? Undoubtedly. Today's example was the case of care workers in the private sector whose employers allowed only five minutes for travel between the homes of clients. As some rural homes were a 25 minute drive apart, the workers' earnings could be reduced thereby to as low as £1 per hour. A good case for collective action.

Naval officers of my generation generally acquired a dislike of unions and Nicolas Monserrat's autobiography indicates why that was sometimes justified. Until Hitler attacked the Soviet Union, trade unions with communist sympathies wanted Britain to lose the war because that might offer a chance of seizing power. But that was then.

Years later in civilian life in Australia my team had members of four unions: for professional engineers, technicians, tradesmen and a solitary clerk. The unions all had one thing in common, expressed by their district officers: if agreement on any issue was reached within the Bureau that was all that mattered.

Only once in seven years did a national dispute overrule that attitude and a 'work to rule' by the Technical Officers was imposed from on high. My mob therefore banned 'packing, loading and driving'.

These activities were essential to supporting field work throughout Australia but I couldn't complain because those tasks were not part of their Job Descriptions. They were merely done on a commonsense basis. A bit of readjustment, other staff to do the packing and loading, some train travel instead of driving. The work went on, unaffected.

It all depends on what kind of unions! Support the best.

Voting. Here's another example of principle and pragmatism. As recorded earlier, voting is one of the four essentials of Australian citizenship and it is compulsory. In practice that means that, firstly: anyone who will not be in their home constituency on polling day must be able to register their votes for that constituency wherever they happen to be. So three weeks before polling day ballot papers for all the constituencies are made available in town and city centre polling stations all over Australia, and the completed papers are double sealed and sent to the relevant constituency.

Secondly, compulsory voting requires papers to be made available to people in hospital, on remand in custody, the armed services wherever they are serving, and overseas. I had to ask to be excused voting now that I'm living 'permanently' in England: I thought it improper to vote when I'm out of touch with Australian affairs.

Finally, enforcement is essential if the requirement is to be taken seriously. Anyone who fails to vote can expect a 'Please explain' letter and, unless they have a good explanation they can be sure a fine will follow.

It was interesting to work for a couple of weeks with other retired professional men and some working-age women in the pre-polling office in Canberra during Federal elections. The women cunningly manipulated the queuing in the hope of getting charming TV presenters and other celebrities to their desk. Less charming, when a half-sozzled Hell's Angel arrived they made sure he came to my desk. He asked if I would be quick because he was going to 'chuck up', the others were amused when I told him firmly to 'Go and get it over and then vote', and he trotted off like a lamb.

Compulsory voting is particularly good for countries with large immigrant populations, especially for those immigrants who have never had the privilege. But I wouldn't recommend Britain to take on the additional expense in this time of austerity.

War and terrorism. I can only add two observations to the flood of news items on these vital matters.

The first is that despite the flood of information since the invasion of Iraq, it has not *felt* as though the country is at war. War, as understood by anyone who was a child in a bombed city during WW2 not only involved fearing for the safety of family members in harms way overseas or on the seas, but also going to bed or the air raid shelter wondering if you would still be alive in the morning. The recent wars seem to have affected only the limited number of families tragically touched by the loss or injury of a member or friend. For most it has been largely unnoticed: shopping and football as usual.

A by-product of wars. Writing during the Vietnam War, an American professor recorded that he had analysed all the history and literature relating to the anti-war protests. He concluded that despite the widespread furore there were only two strategic options to prevent or limit the spread of communism: 'war' and 'containment'. Many years later this prompted a discussion with an older man whom I respected. We set ourselves the question, 'Which of the wars since 1939 absolutely *had* to be fought by Britain'.

We concluded that only WW2 satisfied that criterion. Containment – admittedly backed by one abortive US air strike against him - had worked to prevent the unstable but oil-rich Gaddafi from nuclear Libyan adventures. The Egyptians and Afghans had dislodged the Russians from their countries. When the communist government came to power in China they showed no wish to join Stalin in his ambition to convert the world. Containment and 'carrying a big stick' have kept North Korea in check thus far.

It's sad that we can never know whether the world would have been more peaceful if containment had been tried more widely: Vietnam is the obvious example. Sadder still that the barbaric Islamic State seems unlikely to leave the United Nations any option except a war that *has* to be fought, probably with British participation.

What does it all add up to?

Coming back now to the big picture. During a week spent with a seismic survey team in the Australian bush 200 km west of Alice Springs, I visited the Hermansburg Mission. There I was told that, when houses were built for them, Aboriginal families had chopped up doors for firewood. 'Uncivilised' some would say! But think about it: their basic human needs for shelter, clothing and food were met. So why rush about?

Let's make a fire to keep us warm when the sun goes down, sit around it, tell stories and draw pictures about our historical and spiritual heritage, the 'dream time'. Where's the nearest firewood? Who needs doors? One up for the stone-age, hunter-gatherer culture which populated Australia sustainably for over 40,000 years.

At the opposite end of the scale, many affluent, Western families, especially but not only the working mums, feel hard pressed to balance their work and home lives. It's worse if they have no job or their job is not secure. Worse still, if an employer uses the threat of losing a job to apply pressure to make employees work harder, longer or for less pay.

If lucky enough to be buying their home, the families worry about the mortgage. They complain of the stress involved in earning enough money to meet their own and their children's expectations. Some even worry about climate change. Women, and now increasingly men, are encouraged by marketing to aspire to a magazine photo image of a body without which, they may be encouraged to believe, there can be no self confidence. So they invest in paints, potions, visits to costly gyms and, increasingly, to cosmetic surgery clinics. And worry, worry, worry.

Do the aboriginal and contemporary extremes have anything in common? Seven concepts are, I suggest, shared: shelter, clothing, food, a code of social conduct, medicine, intellectual stimulation and a belief system. And if there are common factors, a 'Third Way' between the above extremes should be possible, despite the conventional wisdom that entrepreneurial enterprise – human greed by another name, perhaps - will prevent any such way becoming stable.

This was never intended to be a scholarly treatise. I have not had time to do more than dip into the 'Third Way' literature. However, the feeling that I have extracted from my samples suggests that the authors were often writing within the context of a belief in continuing growth.

My conviction is that given all the problems we face, especially those which can be labelled 'conspicuous consumption' it would be wise to reduce the rate of depletion of the earth's resources and the accompanying pollution of the air, rivers and seas. Reductions, if on the right scale, would be an insurance against the dismal prospect of discovering a few years hence that the scientists' modelling was right, and that climate change threatens the very existence of our Goldilocks zone.

And what is the right scale? It's quite easy to suggest an answer. It's the scale at which the earth's resources would be sufficient to sustain human life indefinitely. Estimates suggest that at least 2.6 earths would be required at a typical current 'western' consumption rate. So we could assess what proportion of the earth's burden is the result of our UK way of life, by comparing GDP's or some other suitable measure, and then set ourselves the target of 'living within the earth's means'.

Britain cannot solve the world's problems. It is not Britain's responsibility to do so. But we can play a useful part and it really would be great if the country could set a good example to the rest of the world. How might it work? We managed for many years before explicit personal or business 'visions' became trendy but perhaps it's not a bad idea to state one here.

My Vision

My vision is of an egalitarian Britain, in which, in this second decade of the 21st century, despite being an affluent Western nation, we choose to 'learn to live with less'. This would involve rejecting materialistic consumerism and compensating for the resultant decline of inessential elements of the economy by learning to share the remaining, vital, work equably.

In addition to the obvious reduction in unemployment and some of the associated 'benefits' problems, there should be other beneficial consequences. People would have a short working week, three days perhaps, more time to spend with their families, hopefully improving relationships between parents and children. It would allow them, if they wished, to grow food locally, using methods ranging from window boxes to sophisticated new agricultural methods: goodbye manicured lawns, hello vegetables, even goodbye pet rabbits, hello more rabbit pie. Consumption of resources would decrease significantly. So would 'stress'.

Could it happen?

Is the vision Utopian? Somewhat perhaps. However, I recognise the history of failed attempts to establish idealistic cultures and certainly wouldn't want

Huxley's 'welfare-tyranny Utopia'. But it seems more sensible to aim for something better than the drift towards the inevitable destination of the 'Growth' which is deemed so important by many conventional capitalist economists, politicians and businessmen. And the prospect of resource exhaustion and the adverse effects of climate change within a few decades should provide us with more urgent, motivation not to fiddle while Rome burns.

Who would suffer from the proposed changes? At the personal level: any remaining, 'Don't you know who I am?' egos; those brought up to feel entitlement to unearned privileges of one kind or another; and the uberrich who will find it harder to get servants and suppliers. At the family level travel, especially by air would be reduced, world wide gap-year excursions might have to be sacrificed. In the business sector, those who supply and support ultra-affluent, materialistic lifestyles: symbolised for me by the £2,500 to £50,000 range of handbags - does anyone really *need* them?

Those and other frivolities would wither on the vine if we simply refused to succumb to the pressure of 'the markets' and their advertising, and only worked to meet more modest real *needs*. Who would weep if the immediate reward was increased leisure for us all, and the long term reward a sustainable future for our descendants?

What about demographics? Whether or not we aim for a better way of life, the expanding population is one of our biggest problems. Unless our way of living changes, it seems inevitable that older people will suffer hardship because there will not be enough tax-paying workers to support retirement pensions and care for the ageing. So would it not be better if all who are fit enough share the essential work, pay taxes accordingly, limit their material aspirations (and those of their children!), are less stressed, and have more time for their children and their 'olds'?

To answer that question, I hope so. Some thinkers are already suggesting how a reduced number of younger people might support the bulge of aged folk. And no, I haven't forgotten that the key to many aspects of the foregoing ideas is increased, initially at least, funding. I end with the hope that economists will define the ideas more clearly, putting in some figures, and modelling the possibilities to predict whether a stable state at lower levels of activity could be achievable. The changes we need to make will not be easy. They should therefore be gradual but there should be no doubt about the direction of travel nor of our destination.

Speak louder please New Economics Foundation and the other economics 'Think Tanks'. And would the government please be brave enough to present the case for a sustainable future to the nation?

Whether on not the ideas outlined here are of any use at all, I've enjoyed putting them on paper and, I hope, showing them to be, whether over-optimistic or over-pessimistic, at least reasonably coherent.

Final Focus

Continue to

Think Global, Act Local

And add

Learn To Live With Less.

Before it's too late!

Relevant reading

Affluenza. Oliver James

Animal Spirits. Akerlof and Shiller

Aspects of Aristocracy. David Cannadine

Capital: *in the Twenty First Century*. Thomas Picketty

CHAVS: *The Demonisation of the Working Class.* Owen Jones

Citizen Sailors. Glyn Prysor

Class in Australia. Craig Mcgregor

Cold War Command. Richard Woodman and Captain Dan Conley

Conundrum. Jan Morris

Debt: *The First 5,000 Years.* David Graeber

Do Good Lives Have to Cost the Earth? Edited Andrew Simms and Joe Smith

Generations. Hugh Mackay

Growth Isn't Possible. Prof Smith

Guns, Germs and Steel. Jared Diamond

Happiness. Richard Layard

Here on Earth. Tim Flannery

Honest to God. John Robinson the Bishop of Woolwich

Lions Donkeys and Dinosaurs. Lewis Page

Naught for Your Comfort. Father Trevor Huddlestone

Paradise and Power. Robert Kagan

Private Island. James Meek

Prosperity Without Growth. Tim Jackson

Round About a Pound a Week. Maud Pember Reeves

Rudyard Kipling's Verse 1885 – 1926.

Six Degrees: *Our Future on a Hotter Planet*. Mark Lynas

The Better Angels of Our Nature. Steven Pinker

The Elephant and the Flea. Charles Handy

The Establishment: *And How they get Away With It*. Owen Jones

The God Delusion. Richard Dawkins

The Habsburg Café. A P Riemer

The Hungry Spirit. Charles Handy

The Master Mariner. Nicholas Monsarrat

The Truth About Markets. John Kay

Who Owns Britain? Kevin Kahills